Praise for *Overworked and Overwhelmed*

"If I had to choose one skill that could simultaneously bring greater happiness in life and more meaningful engagement in work, it wouldn't be a time management tip, or a productivity hack, or a communication strategy. It would be simple mindfulness. With so many demands on our attention every moment of the day, it's paramount to learn how to direct our attention in order to achieve our highest purposes. There's a way out of the overwhelming busyness of modern life—Scott Eblin has written the guidebook."

—Daniel H. Pink,
New York Times best-selling author of *Drive* and *To Sell Is Human*

"Conscious capitalism begins with consciousness in you. No matter how stressful your work is, *Overworked and Overwhelmed* will show you how to stay present so you can achieve your higher purpose."

—John Mackey,
co-CEO and cofounder of Whole Foods Market
and coauthor of *Conscious Capitalism*

"If the title of *Overworked and Overwhelmed* reminds you of someone you know, stop what you're doing and read this book. Scott Eblin demystifies mindfulness so that you can put it to work and create a better life. With simple and practical guidance based on timeless principles, he shows that if you want to give to others, you have to give to yourself first."

—Adam Grant,
Wharton School professor and *New York Times* best-selling
author of *Give and Take*

"This is indeed a timely book. In a world where high velocity performance is the norm, often, a caffeine-driven, sleep-deprived, smart phone–addicted existence is an inevitable consequence. Scott teaches us that it need not be that way. With simple techniques and routines of mindfulness and self-management, he offers solutions that allow you to come back from the brink. Using his practices, you are likely to find yourself having more capacity as well as feeling more fulfilled and productive. If you want to reclaim yourself, this book is a must-read."

—Raghu Krishnamoorthy,
Vice President, Executive Development and
Chief Learning Officer, General Electric Corporation

"Scott Eblin's must-read book gives you the tools to balance life with work, satisfaction with success, and mindfulness with purpose. Based on years of critical research in leadership success, *Overworked and Overwhelmed* will fundamentally change how you live each day. Brilliant!"

—**Marshall Goldsmith,**
author of the *New York Times* and global best-seller
What Got You Here Won't Get You There

"Increase sales, get leaner, do better, stay connected. *Overworked and Overwhelmed: The Mindfulness Alternative* helps put the demands of corporate life into perspective by providing mindful ways to perform at your best in all aspects of life. Scott Eblin's personal story is inspirational and his approach can help you find new paths to achievement while bringing more meaning into your life."

—**Mark Ronk,**
Head of Learning, Organizational Development and
Talent Management, Nestlé USA

"Most of the leaders I work with, at all levels, are trying to figure out how to manage today's demands of faster, cheaper, and better. In Scott's new book, *Overworked and Over-whelmed: The Mindfulness Alternative*, he helps us see how to work differently. It's about raising our awareness and setting intention. Thank you, Scott, for providing us with such a simple and practical road map that will help anyone who wants to show up at work and home as the best version of themselves."

—**Bob Andrews,**
Director Executive, Coaching, Gap Inc.

"My long-time interest in mindfulness has led me to many fascinating books by Zen monks and academic scholars. However, I'm not planning to live my life on a mountain top or in an ivory tower, and the advice they offered was practically impossible to apply to a life in the fast lane. Scott Eblin knows my world. And he's provided a simple road map and tools that make mindful living in the business world not only possible but easy and fun."

—**Deb Giffen,**
Director, Innovative Learning Solutions,
Wharton Executive Education, and creator of *Nano Tools for Leaders*

"The wisdom in the book is essential and timely. Scott offers a happy and hopeful answer to the question that besets so many of us, 'How can I stop feeling so overworked and overwhelmed?' His practical answer lives in providing proven routines of mindfulness that can truly make a life-saving difference."

—**Marilee Adams, PhD,**
best-selling author of
Change Your Questions, Change Your Life: 10 Powerful Tools for Life and Work

"This book's moment of truth is when the reader becomes aware that there are other ways to define the outcomes and activities of work. With these new intentions, readers will make better personal choices that enhance their emotional commitment to work and leaders will create more abundant organizations that deliver both meaning and money. Scott does a superb job melding personal, coaching, and organization experiences into pragmatic guidelines that will help people become both more aware and more intentional."

—**Dave Ulrich,**
Rensis Likert Professor of Business,
University of Michigan,
Partner, The RBL Group,
and coauthor of *The Why of Work*

overworked

and

overwhelmed

SCOTT EBLIN

overworked
and
overwhelmed

[the mindfulness alternative]

WILEY

As always, for Diane

CONTENTS

Introduction   *Overworked and Overwhelmed?:*
Welcome to the Mindfulness
Alternative   *xv*

Part One

1   *Reality Bites (or Does It?): Why You Feel So*
Overworked and Overwhelmed   *3*

2   *What Does* Mindfulness *Even Mean Anyway?:*
It's Simpler Than You Probably Think   *15*

3   *What's Going on in There, and What Can You*
Do About It?: What You Need to Know About Your
Mind-Body Operating System   *31*

Part Two

4   *Where Do You Want to Go?: Guiding Yourself with a*
Life GPS   *47*

5   *How Are You at Your Best?: Clarifying Your*
Version of Peak Performance   *59*

6 *What's Their Secret?: The One Commitment You Have to Make to Yourself and How to Keep It*   77

Part **Three**

7 *You Are What You Repeatedly Do: How the Right Routines (for You) Help You Show Up at Your Best*   103

8 *It Starts with the Body: The Physical Routines That Make You More Mindful*   115

9 *A Beautiful Mind: The Mental Routines That Reduce Clutter and Increase Focus*   131

10 *In Right Relationship: The Relational Routines That Connect You with the Bigger Picture*   151

11 *What's Your Purpose Here, Anyway?: The Spiritual Routines That Build Perspective*   173

12 *Making It Work: Tips for Following Through (And for Rapid Recovery When You Don't)*   193

Part **Four**

13 *What Are You in It For?: Clarifying Your Outcomes at Home, at Work, and in the Community*   207

14 *Continuing with Your Mindfulness Alternative: Some Lessons Learned for Your Journey* *223*

Appendix: Coach's Corner Compendium *237*

Notes *243*

Acknowledgments *249*

About the Author *253*

Index *255*

Introduction Overworked and Overwhelmed? Welcome to the Mindfulness Alternative

The Backstory

It was 7:30 on a Sunday night on the campus of one of the world's best-known companies, and I was the guest speaker for a group of about 80 of the company's top high potentials. They had just finished the first week of a two-week leadership development program that wrapped up with a weekend project two hours earlier. Week two was set to start the next morning at 8:00 AM. So, it was the time slot that every guest speaker covets, right? (In retrospect, I was lucky to be there at all. Just two years earlier when I made the first presentation I ever gave to leaders in this company, I doubted if I was even going to be able to physically stand long enough to deliver the talk. We'll get to that later.)

My goal that night was to offer up a few ideas and tools that these leaders could use immediately to get stuff done and still have a life. I dived right in by asking the group if they were interested in seeing the results of some leadership behaviors research that I had conducted with a couple of hundred executives in their company. High-achieving people almost always enjoy comparing themselves to a norm, so this group of high-potential leaders was immediately hooked. As I shared the slide for the most highly self-assessed behaviors for their company execs, we looked at a graph that was all about accountability, open communication, and making timely decisions. The headline I shared with the group was, "Leaders here are great at getting stuff done." All the heads in the room nodded up and down. Then we took a look at the lowest self-assessed behaviors. My flipside headline was, "And you're so busy getting stuff done, that you probably don't see what needs to be done." I got more than nodding heads at that point. I got an eruption of emotion.

A catharsis began as the screen showed low rated leadership behaviors such as:

- Pacing myself by building in regular breaks from work
- Regularly taking time to step back to define or redefine what needs to be done
- Giving others my full presence and attention in meetings and conversations

Everyone in that room had a track record of success. And almost everyone in the room talked about their fears that they weren't going to be able to keep it up. They talked about staying late at the office day after day. They talked about the expectation to be "corporate warriors," to always be available, to get by on four hours of sleep a night, to answer e-mails immediately, including in the middle of the night. They all agreed that they were burning out fast.

The exception was a woman in the center of the room who was listening attentively but not contributing to the conversation. She was projecting a sense of calm that stood in stark contrast to the frustration and angst that most of her colleagues were expressing. I asked her what she was thinking. She said, "I'm thinking I don't do any of that stuff." After her colleagues picked their jaws up from the tables, the questions began—How do you do that? How do you pull it off?

Her answer was simple. "I decided a long time ago that I was going to have a life and not just a work life. Unless it's a true emergency, I leave the office every night at 6:00 PM. And, once I get home, I don't answer e-mails. The people who need to reach me know my number. They'll call me if they need me, but I don't answer e-mails all night." From the corner of the room, one of the guys who had been driving the conversation said, "Yeah, because the first time you answer an e-mail at 2:30 in the morning, they know they've got you." Everyone else nodded their heads knowingly.

By definition, this woman was among the top performing leaders in her company. She would not have been in the room if she wasn't. What set her apart from her colleagues was a measure of mindfulness in how she approached her work and her life.

The Purpose of This Book

This book, *Overworked and Overwhelmed: The Mindfulness Alternative*, is for the rest of the people who were in the room that evening. Chances are, if you're reading this, you could have been there that night. As I was writing this book and talking with leaders and other high-capacity professionals about the project, the most common question I got after sharing that the title was *Overworked and Overwhelmed* was, "When can I read it?"

That was encouraging but not surprising. In close to 15 years of work with the top executives and high-potential leaders in scores of the world's best known companies and organizations, I've seen a clear trend develop year over year. Leaders and other professionals are working harder and harder. The input is coming in far faster than any reasonable expectation of output. Too many leaders and professionals today feel overwhelmed by the seemingly nonstop demands on their time and attention. The convergence of 24/7 smartphone connectivity and the permanent restructuring that followed the financial crisis of 2008 have created an environment in which many professionals feel like they're on a gerbil wheel with no way off.

They operate in environments in which the expectations for results are always rising and always changing. Different results require different actions, and all too often, the response of high-achieving people is to do more of what they've been doing. They (you) can't work any harder. They (you) are already maxed out. There are only 168 hours in a week and they're working most of them. There's not a lot of extra margin for them to work more or harder. They need an alternative. That's what this book offers—the mindfulness alternative. This book is a guide to learning to work differently—mindfully—so you are more clear about the results that most merit your time and attention and how you need to show up to offer your highest and best contribution as a professional and as a person.

Jon Kabat-Zinn, the originator of Mindfulness-Based Stress Reduction therapy, has asked, "Sure, mindfulness is difficult, but what's the alternative?"[1] When you think about it, the alternative to mindful living is mindless living. Because of ever changing expectations, the amount of incoming input and the conflicting demands on their time and attention, too many professionals are practicing mindless living. Okay, so mindfulness is the opposite of mindlessness, but what is it? We'll answer that question in depth in Chapter 2, but for now my short and simple definition is that mindfulness is the intersection of two qualities: awareness and intention. By awareness, I mean awareness of what's going on both around you and inside of you in any given moment. Being aware enables you to act in the moment with the intention of creating a particular outcome or result.

The purpose of *Overworked and Overwhelmed* is to make the practice of mindfulness easy, accessible, and relevant for people who feel like they're trapped on the gerbil wheel. The goal is not to turn you into a Buddhist monk or nun but to offer the knowledge that, along with simple, practical, and applicable routines, will help you align your work and the rest of your life with the results that matter most. The emphasis here is on small steps that, when taken consistently over time, lead to big results. If this book helps you raise your effectiveness and improve the quality of your life by 5 percent in the next month, I will consider that a win. Five percent may not sound like much, but if you have a 5 percent improvement each month, in six months you're going to be 30 percent better. That's nothing to sneeze at. Based on my own experience and that of many of my clients, I know you can do it.

Why Me?

If I were you, I might be interested in being less overworked and overwhelmed but would also be asking the question, "Why should I pay attention to what this guy is offering?" Let me attempt to answer that question with two quick stories. One has been public for years, and the other, until the publication of this book, has been very private.

The Public Story

Over the past seven years, I've shared many of the concepts and techniques that will be highlighted in *Overworked and Overwhelmed* with senior and emerging leaders in some of the world's most prominent companies and organizations.

Based on the leadership behaviors research I've conducted with thousands of leaders in these organizations and dozens of others, I've concluded that a more mindful approach to leadership and professional life is desperately needed. Over the past several years, I've been much more explicit in my senior executive coaching engagements and education sessions with high-potential leaders that professionals today are so busy doing things that they often don't see what needs to be done. I'm getting universal agreement with this premise and great success in sharing basic mindfulness routines and habits with executives and other professionals who are hungry for approaches to their work that are effective and more sustainable than the 24/7 expectations that many of them have set for themselves.

My own professional journey includes 15 years of managerial and executive experience in the public sector, work in financial services, and time spent as a vice president in a Fortune 250 energy company. I've spent the past 14 years as a leadership coach, speaker, educator, and author working with C-suite and other senior executives and high-potential leaders in some of the world's best known companies and organizations.

The fact that I'm not a Buddhist monk or the secular equivalent actually makes me well positioned to write this book. Like you, I'm someone who is leading a very fast paced life. I run a successful business. I have a family. I have friends and interests outside of work. I live in a bustling city, not a retreat center in Big Sur. I've had my share of ups and downs. Sometimes I'm proud of the way I show up, and other times I'd love to have a do-over. In short, I'm just a guy who's doing the best he can and trying to figure things out.

For more than 20 years, though, I've worked diligently to incorporate mindfulness into my life. I didn't even think of it as mindfulness when I started out. As I've learned more over time, though, that's what I've been trying to do.

My mindfulness journey includes 20 years of annual reflection and planning retreats with my wife, Diane, 15 years of regular (more or less) meditation and prayer, more than 1,200 yoga classes in the past four years, and the recent completion of a 200-hour training program that led to me becoming a Registered Yoga Teacher.

The Private Story

That previous line about completing a yoga teacher training program is the setup for the private version of the story about why you may want to consider me as your guide on this journey to a more mindful way of living and working.

In the summer of 2009, I was diagnosed with multiple sclerosis (MS). That was one of the great shocks of my life, as I was 48 years old, had run two marathons, and thought I was in excellent health and pretty much bulletproof.

My self-identity in 2009 often started with "I'm a runner." I started running when I was 13 years old. Although I was never that fast, I had a lot of endurance and would regularly run for an hour or more at a time. Beginning in late 2008, that got increasingly harder to do. With each passing week, my legs felt more and more like they had lead weights in them. Then I started getting lower back pain. Like any good twenty-first-century professional, I got on WebMD and tried to self-diagnose. My conclusion was a condition called lumbar stenosis in which a bone spur on your spine presses against a nerve. I thought this would be easy to fix so I went to a physiatrist to get my diagnosis confirmed and start treatment. She suggested I get some MRI scans taken of my spine and come back in two weeks.

Two weeks later, I went back to see her. As I was walking across the parking lot from my car to her office that day I could feel my feet getting numb. Early in our time together, the doctor told me that the MRIs showed lesions on my spinal cord, that she thought I had multiple sclerosis, and that I should see a neurologist. To make a long story short, the neurologist ran all the requisite tests, and sure enough, I had MS.

The rest of 2009 was downhill from there. Within a few weeks I could barely walk around the block and had to sort of pull myself by the banister to walk upstairs to my bedroom. A couple of months after the diagnosis, I was in downtown Washington, D.C., for a meeting. As I was leaving, a huge summer storm broke out of nowhere. I tried to run for my car, which was four blocks away, and couldn't feel my feet. Pretty tough for someone whose self-identity was "I'm a runner." The story that began to replace "I'm a runner" was "the great crippler of young adults." (I recently learned that this line came from an old Barbra Streisand public service announcement for MS that I must have seen a lot as a kid.)

A month later, I was scheduled to give my first ever presentation to that major global company that I referred to at the beginning of this introduction. A week before the event, I said to Diane, "I think I'm going to be doing that speech with a cane." It turns out that I didn't need a cane that day, but I didn't allow myself to get more than a couple of feet away from the podium in case I needed to grab it on the way down.

Later that year, my brain started feeling like a wet sponge inside my skull. I was afraid to go see clients because I wasn't even making sense to myself. I was losing thoughts and words. I could barely walk, let alone run. Early in 2010, I enrolled in a trial at Johns Hopkins Medical Center for a new MS drug. I was told the side effects of the biweekly injections would be flulike symptoms for a few hours. That was true at first. Then the symptoms extended for a day, then a weekend, and then three or four days at a time. After each injection, I was flat on my back for a longer period of time. It got to the point where Diane would have to help me lift my head off the couch to take a drink of water.

She was desperate to help me and in October 2010 encouraged me to start going to yoga on the off weeks from the injections. I was amazed that I could do it at all. It made me feel so much better that I quickly became a regular. On a Monday in December of that year, I got a call from my doctor at Hopkins. He told me that based on my blood work from the prior week, I needed to get to Baltimore right away so he could admit me to the hospital. I told him that I had spent the previous afternoon in a three hour yoga workshop and asked how I could possibly need to be admitted. In return he asked, "Do you want to hear your page numbers?" My markers of normal liver functions were 10 times higher than they should have been. With each injection of the MS drug, my liver moved closer to failure.

While the drugs work for many people, they didn't work for me. It was at that point that I stopped taking them and started doing yoga four or five times a week. I learned a lot more about what I should and shouldn't eat to keep my autoimmune system healthy. I got more serious about meditation. Six months after I almost had liver failure, I did the first headstand I had ever done in my life—and that was just a few weeks before my fiftieth birthday. Today, I practice yoga six or seven times a week, have completed that 200-hour yoga teacher training, and do some combination of headstands, handstands, and arm balances pretty much every day. While the physical strength and flexibility I've gained has been vitally important to managing my health, the perspective and calm that I've built through the practice is equally important. I'm stronger than I've ever been and savoring each moment of life in a way that I never have before.

Pursuing the mindfulness alternative literally saved my life. If you've read this far, I believe it can save yours. That's why I've written this book. I am so glad you're here.

How We'll Roll

Overworked and Overwhelmed is organized into four parts.

Part One has three goals: to define the nature and sources of the overworked and overwhelmed state you find yourself in, to lay out the choice between mindful and mindless living, and to open up the hood on your brain and body to share some information about your operating system and how to manage it.

The goal of Part Two is to start painting the picture of what your version of non-overworked and non-overwhelmed success would look like. I'll introduce you to the Life GPS® personal planning model that will be the organizing framework for the rest of this book. We'll get a running start on answering the first of three big questions framed by the Life GPS: "How do you show up when you're performing at your best?" And we'll wrap up Part Two by taking a reality-check look at the one commitment you have to make for any aspect of the mindfulness alternative to work. (You can do it. I know you can.)

In Part Three, we'll answer the second big Life GPS question: "What are the simple, practical, and immediately applicable routines that will enable you to show up at your best?" Those routines fall into four domains: physical, mental, relational, and spiritual. There are lots of great routines you can adopt in any or all of those areas that will help you strengthen the mindfulness muscles that will enable you to feel less overworked and overwhelmed. The fact is, though, that you probably don't have time for a lot of new routines in your life. That's why each of the routine chapters will focus on a Killer App—that one thing you should do if you're not going to do anything else in that domain. If you're interested in doing a little more, you'll find short Habit Hacks throughout Part Three that are relatively easy to do and likely to make a difference. Recognizing that none of us are perfect, Part Three will finish up with some ideas on how to keep the wheels on your bus and how to get back on the road quickly when the wheels come off.

Part Four will help you pull it all together by sparking your thoughts and intentions around the last of the three big Life GPS questions: "If you're regularly showing up at your mindful best, what are the results and outcomes you hope to see in the three big arenas of life—your life at home, your life at work, and your life in your broader community?"

Every chapter will end with a Coach's Corner, where I'll ask a few questions that will help you identify your takeaways from each chapter and how they apply to you.

So, are you sick of being overworked and overwhelmed? Are you ready for the mindfulness alternative? Awesome. Let's keep going.

Part One

1 Reality Bites (or Does It?)

Why You Feel So Overworked and Overwhelmed

Does Any of This Sound Familiar?

At a breakfast joint in L.A., my friend John was telling me about the first full day of his business trip to the West Coast. John and his partner own a successful strategy consulting firm that they started in 2009 right in the teeth of the Great Recession. Since then, through business savvy and a lot of hard work, they've acquired an impressive list of clients and built a team of 10 really smart people. Much of their success can be attributed to days like the one John had the day before our breakfast meeting.

What You'll Learn in This Chapter:

- Why you feel overworked and overwhelmed
- Why things feel crazier lately
- Why being present matters and what you can do about it

"So, here's my day yesterday," he began. "I'm up at 6:00 AM and in the rental car by 7:00 AM for a drive from my hotel in West Hollywood to an 8:30 meeting in East L.A. Of course, that drive could be anywhere from 45 minutes to an hour and a half depending on the traffic on the freeways. About 20 minutes into the drive, I hear, 'Cheep! Cheep! Cheep!' It's the phone. I get on a conference call while I'm driving that includes a client dialing in from Denmark. I sort of have this out-of-body experience while I'm driving, thinking, 'How absurd is this that I'm driving at 7:30 AM somewhere in L.A. while I'm talking to people in D.C. and Denmark?' So, the call finishes, and I get to East L.A. a few minutes before the meeting begins. It's an all-day session to close out a big project with a major client. Fortunately, it goes well, and by the end of the day, we've probably won some new business. Handshakes all around, and I get back in the car just after 4:00 PM. Now I'm driving a colleague to catch a flight back to D.C. out of LAX because she needs to get back to run a marathon on Saturday. Drop her off, take a deep breath, and am finally ready to chill a little bit on the drive back to the hotel in West Hollywood. Then I hear, 'Cheep! Cheep! Cheep!' It's the phone. A guy on the team in D.C. is setting up an emergency conference call to go over a spreadsheet that's critical to another client project. God, it was painful. We go over that spreadsheet cell by cell as I'm navigating the [12 lanes! Be careful, John!] 405 freeway. Finally, I get back to the hotel around 6:30 PM. Grab some dinner. Answer e-mails and prep for today's meetings. Go to bed at 11:00 PM. Typical day on the road."

I had two reactions to John's story. First, I felt bad about asking him to come out to meet me for an 8:00 AM breakfast 45 minutes from his hotel after the day he'd just had. (He was right on time, by the way.) Second, I asked him if I could share his story in this book because it's the perfect representation of what I mean by overworked and overwhelmed.

If my math is right, John clocked around a 17-hour workday as he talked with colleagues and clients, drove around L.A., solved problems, delivered on commitments, developed new business, did favors for friends, responded to requests, stayed current with what was going on, and prepped for the next day's work. And, oh yeah, and found time to feed himself.

Don't get me wrong. Not every single day is like that for John and other high-capacity professionals like him, but many are. Perhaps your typical day doesn't include taking meetings and conference calls all over Los Angeles but is more like Monica Oswald's daily routine:

Monica is a well-respected vice president in a well-known financial services company. She is also a mom with a full and busy life. She and her husband have two kids—a daughter about to graduate from high school and a son in middle school. Her typical day starts at 5:00 AM. She gets up an hour or so ahead of the rest of the family for some "quiet time" while she perhaps does some things in the kitchen or the laundry so, as she told me, she "can get things going" for the day. Of special attention is organizing things for her seventh-grade son, who has a mild learning disability. Monica makes sure "that everything is all where it needs to be so he can pick up and go in the morning."

Her next move is to drop her son off at the bus stop, and then she's in her office between 7:00 and 7:30 AM. She tries to take the first 60 to 90 minutes of the workday to organize herself, answer e-mails, make follow-up calls, review her calendar, and set her priorities for the day. At 8:30 or 9:00 AM, the meetings begin and pretty much continue throughout the day. As we'll hear more about from Monica later in this book, she takes a 20-minute walk outside or around the building around midday to get a physical and mental break from sitting in conference rooms.

If no evening events are planned at work, she's typically home by 6:00 PM, unless one of the kids has a school event. If not, then it's dinner and helping her son with his homework. She tries to wrap things up by 9:00 PM, check a few e-mails, and attend to anything she needs to with the goal of being in bed by 10:00 PM and asleep by 11:00 PM. Then, as she told me, "it starts again."

Like I said, a full and busy life. Don't get me wrong; from talking with her, I can tell that Monica loves her family, her job, and her life. Still, that's a lot to keep up with on a daily basis.

As I've been working on this book, I've been sharing some ideas from it with clients and friends who, like John and Monica, are in demanding leadership or other professional roles. When I share the title of the book with them, it's usually what I call a Jerry McGuire moment—"You had me at hello." As soon as most people hear the first three words of the title, *Overworked and Overwhelmed,* the reaction is something along the lines of "When can I read it?" or "Can I read it while you're writing it?" My favorite response was from an executive who, when she heard the title, exclaimed, "Oh my gosh, if I had that book, I'd jump in bed with it and not get out until I finished it!"

The Situations You Find Yourself In . . .

If you're reading this book, chances are you feel the same way (although I won't press you on where you're reading it). Why is it that so many professionals feel so overworked and overwhelmed? If you're like almost all the people I work with, it's because your calendar is racked and stacked with very little white space between all of the work, family, and community commitments on your plate. But is that calendar the cause or the effect of being overworked and overwhelmed?

These are questions I've been paying a lot of attention to over the past five or six years. During that time, I've given an average of 40 to 50 presentations a year to groups of high-potential and senior leaders who read my first book, *The Next Level: What Insiders Know About Executive Success.* When I first wrote that book, the next level I most had in mind was making the transition from manager to a more senior manager or executive role. That's clearly a next-level situation, but the more I talked with people, the more I realized that just about everyone in executive, managerial, or other high-capacity professional roles is experiencing next-level situations on an almost continuous basis, whether they've been recently promoted or not.

Let's say we have a roomful of 100 professionals, managers, or executives, and I ask them to raise their hand if they've experienced the following scenarios in the past year:

- *Promotion?* That's usually around 20 percent of the hands.
- *In the same job you were in a year ago but the scope has gotten a lot bigger?* That'll be around 50 percent of the hands.
- *Working in a situation where the performance bar is significantly higher than a year ago?* Ninety to 100 percent of the hands go up.
- *Operating in a rapidly changing competitive environment?* That's 100 percent of the hands.

So, if you're doing the math at home, you've realized that most people are raising their hand more than once. Many of them are raising their hand three and even four times.

. . . And the Denominator They Have in Common

So what do those scenarios have in common that make all of them next-level situations? In all four cases—promotion, increased scope, higher performance bar, and changing competitive environment— different results are expected. When you have to get different results, you need to take different actions. For the majority of leaders and other professionals, their circumstances are compelling them to make lots of changes at once on a nearly continuous basis. Sounds like a pretty good prescription for being overworked and overwhelmed.

The Next Level 360-degree assessments and self-assessments we've run with thousands of managers and executives over the past five years bear this out. When you look at the highest-rated behaviors, they include words like *taking accountability, being clear about outcomes, making timely decisions,* and *correcting mistakes.* It looks a lot like the results for the group whose story I shared in the Introduction, and it's almost always the same story: It's all about getting stuff done.

When you look at the lowest-rated behaviors—the ones that leaders and their colleagues agree they don't do so well—the phrases that come up again and again are *managing my workload, taking time to step back to define or redefine what needs to be done, giving others my full presence and attention.* The behavior that is invariably the lowest rated is *pacing myself by building in regular breaks from work.* If you're reading this book and you're at all similar to the thousands of leaders who have participated in this assessment, the likelihood is that your results would be the same. That's why you feel overworked and overwhelmed.

Why It Feels Crazier Lately

Does it feel like it's gotten worse over the past several years? Most of the people I talk to and work with feel like it has. What's going on in the bigger picture that's driving this? I think there are two macro factors at play. The first is that the corporate restructuring that began with the retrenchment of the Great Recession of 2008 hasn't stopped. As companies downsized to deal with the financial crisis, they learned how to do more with less. That dynamic is enabled by the speed and efficiency of the Internet and other technologies, along with giving more responsibilities to the people who remain. And the people who remain are dealing with the blessing and the curse of the second big factor that emerged in the same period: the rise of the smartphone. The iPhone was introduced in June 2007. As I write this in 2014, there are more than 1 billion smartphones in use around the world.

According to the *MIT Technology Review,* smartphones have had one of the fastest penetration rates of any technology ever introduced.[1] It took only about two and a half years for the smartphone to reach 40 percent market penetration in the United States, compared with around 14 years for the personal computer and 39 years for the Alexander Graham Bell telephone.

And what does the smartphone enable all of us to do? Yes, we can take pictures and share them on Instagram and settle arguments at the bar or dinner table by whipping out the phone and finding the right answer on Google. That can be fun, but the smartphone also enables us to work—all the time. A survey of executives, managers, and professionals (EMPs) conducted by the Center for Creative Leadership in 2013 shows that the typical smartphone-carrying EMP is interacting with work an average of 72 hours a week.[2] That's 43 percent of the 168 hours that are in a week. So, you may be thinking, "Well, that still leaves 57 percent of the week available for other things. That's not so bad." Before you get too excited, though, as the pie chart in Figure 1.1 suggests, you may want to take around eight hours a day for eating, sleeping, and bathing (at least I hope so). When you take the working and personal care out of the mix, that leaves just 24 percent, or 40 hours, of your week available for everything else you want or have to do.

It's no wonder you feel overworked and overwhelmed! In an interview for this book, Teresa Amabile, Harvard Business School professor and coauthor of *The Progress Principle,* summed things up nicely:

> Work is now part of everything we do. We're never away from it. We really have to go to extremes to get away from it. There used to be much clearer demarcations between work and nonwork time. I think because of technology we've come to have higher expectations of each other and of ourselves and of our organizations.

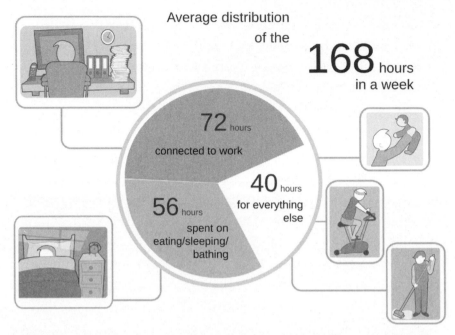

Figure 1.1 Your 168 Hours a Week: Where Do They Go?

Those higher expectations lead to the stress that comes from feeling overworked and overwhelmed. The American Psychological Association's (APA) 2013 Stress Study shows that 33 percent of Americans feel extreme stress and that 48 percent of Americans report their stress has gone up in the past five years.[3] When people were asked why their stress was up, work was the number one reason; concerns about money ranked number two. Those two factors combined were cited by 76 percent of survey participants. When it comes to managing stress, only 29 percent think they do a good job of it and 83 percent think it affects their health. They're right about that last point. According to the Benson-Henry Institute for Mind Body Medicine at Massachusetts General Hospital, between 60 and 90 percent of visits to the doctor are prompted by stress-related complaints.[4]

Even if you're not going to the doctor because of it, there's likely a lot going on in your average day that creates that stress-inducing feeling of being overworked and overwhelmed. For instance, if you're a manager or an executive, according to a January 2012 *Smart Brief on Leadership* reader poll, there's a 96 percent likelihood that you overcommit yourself and your team at least some of the time.[5] You may be a part of the 42 percent who say they overcommit themselves and their teams pretty much all the time. If you're not one of those overcommitting managers or execs, then there's a fair chance you're working for one. Statistics like these make you wonder what kind of self-esteem payoff such overcommitment creates.

Even if you're not a manager or executive, you're almost certainly a professional who uses e-mail. If that's the case, based on the findings of a University of California at Irvine study, you're switching screens on your computer an average of 37 times an hour.[6] That's a screen switch about every 90 seconds. Makes it hard to focus, doesn't it? Another possible reason for lack of focus and a feeling of being overwhelmed is that you deal with a lot of interruptions during the day. A 2011 study out of the Netherlands showed that the engineers in the study were interrupted for an average of 96 minutes a day.[7] What were they able to get done in the midst of all those interruptions? Not as much as they hoped. The urgent and less important work was more likely to be completed than the important work.

Of course, it's not all about work. There are likely other factors in your life that could be making you feel overwhelmed. Another look at the 2013 APA Stress Study suggests what some of those factors might be. Following work pressure and money, the next top five reasons that cause people to feel stressed are health (a vicious circle on that one, huh?), relationships, poor nutrition, media overload (thanks again, smartphone), and sleep deprivation. Sigh.

You Must Be Present to Win

Enough with the statistics; you get the point. If all of these factors sound really familiar, you may even be feeling a little more overworked and overwhelmed at the moment. If that's the case, I apologize. Let's take a few deep breaths (seriously, take a few deep breaths), switch gears, and start focusing on alternatives.

In my line of work as an executive coach and leadership educator, I'm in a lot of conversations about leadership presence. It's sort of the holy grail for leaders these days. Leadership presence is one of those things that everyone wants to exhibit but is hard to define. Believing that it's easier to coach to something for which there is a clear definition, I offered a simple explanation of leadership presence in my first book, *The Next Level*. Based on experience and observation, I believe leadership presence is composed of three big categories of behaviors:

- *Personal presence:* how you view yourself and how others view you
- *Team presence:* how you get things done through and with the team you're accountable for on a day-to-day basis
- *Organizational presence:* how you work outside of your day-to-day team to get bigger things done than you can do on your own

What each of those subsets of leadership presence has in common is that to exercise them you actually have to be present. By *present,* I don't just mean physically present but also mentally, relationally, and even spiritually present. Even if you're not in a formal leadership role in your organization, chances are you serve in other formal or informal leadership roles all the time—at home and in your community. How can you show up with presence when you're so overworked and overwhelmed that you're struggling with even being fully present? The answer is, you can't.

Here's some good news, though. It doesn't have to be that way. One of my favorite definitions of *leadership* is that it's a two part job—the first is to define reality; the second is to offer hope. I think that's also a good definition for my primary profession of leadership coaching and education, as well as for being a good parent, a good friend, a good partner, and the many other roles that most of us end up playing in life.

So we've just spent most of this chapter defining the reality of the overworked and overwhelmed life that so many of us live. What's the alternative that offers hope? That's what the rest of this book is about. As the subtitle of the book suggests, I think the answer lies in developing some level of mindfulness as an alternative to struggling to keep up with the overworked and overwhelmed state in which it's all too easy to find ourselves these days. It's not as hard or as challenging or even as intimidating as it might seem.

Let's get started by unpacking what mindfulness is and isn't in the next chapter.

Coach's Corner

- What's making you feel overworked and overwhelmed?
- What's the payoff for you from overcommitting to many of the things that make you feel overworked and over-whelmed?
- What are the big wedges in your pie chart of how you spend the 168 hours you get each week? What would you like to change about that?
- What are the biggest drivers of distraction that keep you from being fully present?

2 What Does *Mindfulness* Even Mean Anyway?

It's Simpler Than You Probably Think

Mindfulness in the Midst of Disaster

A week after Hurricane Katrina had ravaged the Gulf Coast and the levees had breached and flooded New Orleans, U.S. Coast Guard Admiral Thad Allen flew into the devastated city for the first time. Chaos and suffering had reigned in the first days after the storm, as federal, state, and local leaders were overwhelmed by the scope of the disaster. There had been many examples of heroism performed by rescuers from the Coast Guard, other agencies, and private citizens, but thousands of people were still trapped in their homes a week later,

---

What You'll Learn in This Chapter

- A practical definition of mindfulness
- How mindfulness sets you up for high performance
- Some common barriers to mindfulness

---

bodies were laying in the streets, and a public safety crisis was evolving at the Superdome as storm refugees were trapped there with very little water or food. By the time Admiral Allen was asked by the president to take over the government's response, New Orleans was on the verge of anarchy. Allen's job was to pull the situation back from the brink and to come up with a plan that would accelerate the recovery from the storm.

In an interview for this book, Allen told me what he saw from his helicopter as he approached New Orleans and how that shaped his thinking and approach:

> When we flew in over the city it was still filled with water. The water was black. The odor was pretty intense. The temperature was in the nineties. There was no potable water, no electricity; there was sewage in the town. There were still helicopters buzzing around. Some were trying to repair levees and floodwalls that had collapsed. . . .
>
> When I flew over the city it just struck me like a bolt of lightning that one of the reasons we'd had all the problems in the previous week . . . was that we didn't understand the problem. . . .
>
> We weren't really dealing with the hurricane anymore. [It] was pretty much gone within 48 hours. . . . [What we were dealing with was the] equivalent of a weapon of mass effect used on the city without criminality that resulted in a loss of continuity of government without decapitation of leadership.

With the perspective of watching from a distance what had happened in the previous week and then flying in over the city, Allen was very aware of what he was dealing with. There was no coordination among the officials who would have normally been accountable for disaster recovery. All the communications systems that would have normally allowed them to take control were destroyed by the storm and then by the flooding caused by the broken levees. Allen realized that the impact of the levees failing was essentially the same as if a terrorist group had blown them up in order to wipe out the city with a flood.

With awareness of the nature of the challenge and what it would require from him, Allen then set some intentions around his immediate priorities: to establish a clear chain of command among the agencies that could solve the problems and to assure the citizens of New Orleans that a new level of help was on the way. In his first press conference after arriving, he wanted the people of the city and those watching from around the United States and the world to know that he was aware of the depth of the problems and that he intended to turn things around. He told me:

> The watch words I used . . . were to be completely transparent with the public, to be honest with them, to create expectations of what we were going to do . . . and to let them know that I was there to manage the response. . . . I don't know how many times I said that in my first news conference. "I'm here. I'm accountable."

That press conference marked the beginning of the recovery of New Orleans and the Gulf Coast. Allen was a mindful leader in the right place at the right time. Most of us, no matter how overworked and overwhelmed we are, will ever face the gravity of a situation like the one that Allen faced. But, on a relative basis, we all face our own crises, challenges, and opportunities that call for mindfulness. What can we learn about mindfulness from the way Allen turned things around on the response to Katrina? What does mindfulness even mean anyway?

Mindfulness = Awareness + Intention

In this chapter, we'll hear what some experts have to say about mindfulness and, through the example of Admiral Allen, consider why a practical definition of mindfulness boils down to awareness and intention. We'll also flag the factors that can keep you from performing at your mindful best and then wrap up with why, if you want to pursue the mindfulness alternative, you need to be aware of and ready for your moment of truth and intentional about what comes next.

Mindfulness Begins with Awareness

Jon Kabat-Zinn created the Mindfulness-Based Stress Reduction (MBSR) program at the University of Massachusetts Medical Center in 1979. The program was a groundbreaking combination of mindfulness meditation and yoga that has made dramatic differences for people suffering from chronic pain and anxiety. Over the years, MBSR programs have been established at more than 200 hospitals around the world, and its stress management principles have been adopted in programs conducted by thousands of organizations from Aetna Insurance to Google to the U.S. Army. Kabat-Zinn is a true pioneer in the application of mindfulness in everyday life.

He offered a simple definition of mindfulness in a February 2013 panel discussion for the Nour Foundation when he said, "Mindfulness is the awareness that arises by paying attention on purpose in the present moment and nonjudgmentally."[1] Let's break that down piece by piece:

- *Awareness* is another word for noticing what's going on.
- *Paying attention on purpose* suggests that we can make a choice to be aware and notice.
- *In the present moment* means focusing on what's happening right now, not ruminating on what's already happened or worrying about what might happen.
- *Nonjudgmentally* means we don't waste mental or emotional energy labeling events or thoughts as good or bad. We just acknowledge what we're seeing, thinking, or feeling.

Awareness Leads to Choice and Then Intention

Even if you've never been on a yoga mat yourself, you've probably heard of Power Yoga. It's a vigorous form of yoga that stretches you out, gets your heart rate going, and makes you strong. It was invented in the 1980s by a teacher named Bryan Kest. I'm fortunate to take classes with Kest on a regular basis, and in talking with him for this book, he offered a definition of mindfulness that builds on Kabat-Zinn's definition:

> Mindfulness means being aware of where your mind dwells because it's only [then] that you can stop feeding harmful tendencies. . . . That's what mindfulness is. Wake up. Wake up, and look at what you're doing. . . .
>
> [If you're] conscious of where your mind dwells, then you can decide, "Is that a healthy place? Am I having judgmental thoughts right now? Am I having critical thoughts right now? Angry thoughts? Fearful thoughts? Are the type of thoughts I'm having creating what I want?" . . .
>
> That brings us full circle. That's where mindfulness comes in. You start to notice that [kind of stuff]. When you notice it, then you have a choice in your life.

To sum up, Kest is saying that mindfulness is about waking up and being aware of what you're thinking so that you can assess the impact of your thoughts and then make an intentional choice about what to do next. Mindfulness is about managing that gap between your thoughts and actions.

Human beings are the only species in the animal kingdom who have the capacity to manage that gap. This observation was eloquently and movingly presented by Viktor Frankl in his memoir, *Man's Search for Meaning.*[2] Before he founded the school of psychiatry known as logotherapy, Frankl was a prisoner at Auschwitz and other Nazi death camps. He lost his wife, children, and most of his family in the Holocaust. Rather than allowing that experience to crush him, he gained insights that saved his life and eventually changed the lives of millions of others. One day in camp, after another of the inhuman atrocities inflicted by his guards, Frankl realized that the Nazis could take everything away from him except for one thing—his dignity and sense of worth as a human being. From that moment forward, no matter what his captors did to him, he chose to respond in a way that upheld his dignity. His example began to change the behavior of many of his fellow prisoners and even some of his guards. His choice helped him survive.

Reflecting on his experience in the concentration camps and how his choice saved and changed his life, Frankl wrote, "Between stimulus and response there is a space. In that space is our power to choose our response. In our response lies our growth and our freedom."[3]

How Mindfulness Sets You Up for High Performance

Mindfulness is what fills the space between stimulus and response. Awareness of what's going on externally in the outside world and internally in your mind gives you the insight to choose an intentional response. By accessing the mindfulness alternative, you can choose responses and make decisions that reduce the feeling of being overworked and overwhelmed. As Caroline Starner, the senior vice president of human resources for sunglasses and sports apparel company Oakley, said to me, "Mindfulness is not about clearing your brain; it's about being able to think clearly." The mindfulness alternative is not about sitting with your legs crossed and your eyes closed for hours a day. It's about putting yourself in a position to be more aware and intentional about what's really going on inside and out and what, if anything, you want to do about it.

Teddy Tannenbaum is a longtime student of mindfulness as well as an executive coach and consultant who has spent decades working with executives and managers at well-known companies including

Apple, Disney, and Whole Foods. In a conversation with me, he made this great point about mindfulness, awareness, and intention:

> Mindfulness is not a passive thing. People are afraid, "If I become more mindful I'll be more gentle, more passive. I won't get shit done." No, you'll be more conscious; you'll make better decisions. You'll be more insightful and more incisive, and you're not going to be bound by your biases.

Tannenbaum's point sets us up nicely to come back to the example of Admiral Allen as a mindful leader. No one would ever accuse Allen of being passive. He's focused, direct, and decisive. But because he's aware and intentional, he's also mindful. Let's break down how those two factors manifested in his mindful approach to leading the Katrina recovery effort.

Awareness

Awareness operates in two big domains, external and internal, and one big time frame, right now. When Allen flew into New Orleans after Katrina, he was aware of what was going on externally. To use Harvard leadership expert Ron Heifetz's metaphor of the need for leaders to regularly shift their perspective between the dance floor and the balcony, Allen, as he flew over New Orleans in a Coast Guard helicopter, literally got a balcony view of the situation he was dealing with.[4] Then he showed great internal awareness of how he needed to show up to deal effectively with what he was seeing externally.

Allen's approach very much lined up with leadership (and former tennis) coach Tim Gallwey's definition of *performance*—your performance (*P*) equals your potential (*p*) minus the interference (*i*).[5] It's expressed in this simple equation:

$$P = p - i$$

If you can eliminate the interference, you're left with pure potential. The interference can be either extrinsic or intrinsic. The extrinsic interference is external, and often there is little you can do about it. The facts on the ground in New Orleans and the Gulf Coast were what they were when Allen arrived. There was nothing he could immediately do to change any of that. What mattered most at that point was his ability to recognize and manage his intrinsic or internal response to what he saw as he flew over the city. His mindful capacity to choose his response to what he saw made all the difference.

Intention

That leads to the second part of this two-part definition of mindfulness: intention. Once you're aware of what's going on externally, outside of you, and internally, inside of you, what is the next best choice to intentionally make? In Allen's case, it was to immediately establish clear lines of authority and then to reassure the people of New Orleans that an accountable commander was in place to coordinate the response to the disaster. Being fully aware of what was going on externally and how he needed to respond internally, Allen was able to be intentional about what he needed to do and how he needed to do it.

Through awareness and intention, the mindfulness alternative sets you up for high performance. It helps you identify the difference between extrinsic interference that you can't control and the intrinsic interference of thoughts that can keep you from performing at your full potential. The more you mitigate the intrinsic interference, the more your performance equals your potential.

What Are the Barriers to Mindfulness?

So we'd probably all like to show up and be as calm and cool under pressure as Thad Allen. Heck, we'd probably settle for something that looks like mindfulness in the sixth meeting of the day, in the traffic jam we didn't expect, or with the kids that demand our attention *right now!* How do you build a stance of mindfulness that will serve you well in high-stakes situations as well as in the gerbil wheel of everyday life? That's the question we'll be addressing in the rest of this book.

But first, in the belief that it pays to know your enemy, let's take a quick look at some of the common barriers to mindfulness.

Mental Chatter

Vritti is a Sanskrit word that refers to the chatter in your mind. The Hindus came up with that word thousands of years ago, and if anything, vritti is probably a bigger challenge today than it was then. Another great phrase for this is *monkey mind.* It's the intrinsic interference we were just talking about. It's also what Susan Piver, mindfulness author and founder of the Open Heart Project, calls discursive thinking. She shared with me a funny example of what discursive thinking sounds like inside your head:

> What are your discursive thoughts? Hmm, I wonder what she is talking about. What does *discursive* mean? I should know what that means maybe. I hope it's not cancer. Did anybody go shopping for dinner?

Is there anyone who's not familiar with thoughts bouncing from one seemingly unrelated thing to another? Of course not; we all are. Mental chatter, or intrinsic interference, is a fact of the human condition. The trick is to recognize it when it's happening. By developing the mindfulness alternative, you'll be more aware of the chatter when you hear it and make an intentional choice to reorganize your thinking. As Oakley's Caroline Starner describes it:

It's about a state of being, but it's also the ability to put yourself in that state of being. So I think when you are being mindful, you are aware that your thought processes are chaotic and that you need to do something to break that cycle and return yourself to a calm state where you can function in a better, more high-quality way.

One of Thad Allen's favorite axioms is, "You have to be careful about what rents space in your head." That's the first step in quieting the mental chatter. Being aware of the chatter is the first step to overcoming it.

Distractions

So many things can distract us from focusing on what we really intend to pay attention to. For more than 20 years, Tracy Columbus has led a busy life as a personal manager to actors and other artists. Columbus grew up in Rochester, New York, in the 1960s and 1970s, when Kodak was the flagship employer in town. According to Columbus, people in Rochester were so into cameras back then that they saw very little of what was going on in their lives because they were too busy taking pictures of what was going on in their lives. Of course, that's the analog precursor of constantly taking selfies and other pictures with our smartphones. The distractions don't stop there, of course. How many e-mails and text messages do you get a day? When you're working at your computer, how often do you switch screens? As noted in Chapter 1, the research suggests it's probably about once every 90 seconds. More research from the University of California at Irvine shows that you're likely interrupted once every 11 minutes and that it takes about 25 minutes to get back to the original task you were working on before the interruption.[6] Clearly, the math is not working in our favor when it comes to distractions, so we'll have to come up with some alternatives for dealing with them.

Lack of Awareness in Your Story

There are undoubtedly too many barriers to mindfulness to catalog, so I'll end this section with just one more and that's your awareness—or lack of awareness—about the story you're living in. To keep it simple, I'll break this idea down into two categories of stories: the micro story and the macro story.

The micro story is the story you're telling yourself about whatever is happening right now, whatever happened in the past that seems to affect right now, or whatever might happen in the future. Quite often the story will focus on a specific source of extrinsic interference you're noticing. The real story, though, is whether you recognize the intrinsic interference that the extrinsic interference is creating in your mind. Do you have enough micro story awareness to recognize when you start to go mentally (and even physically) off the rails? We'll talk more about how that happens and what to do about it in the next chapter.

That brings us to your macro story. The macro story is the one you tell yourself about why you're doing what you're doing. Are you even aware you have one? If you aren't, there's a pretty excellent chance that you're living someone else's story and aren't even aware of it.

This idea about living someone else's story really hit home with me a few years ago. I was in charge of a two-day leadership program for high-potential managers at a major corporation, and the group's conversation turned to how hard everyone was working. One of the participants was a really bright and funny regional manager with a big frame and a personality to match. He told us a story about how he and his wife, along with two other couples, took all their kids to the Atlantis resort in the Bahamas for their second trip there in two summers. "So, we're out at the pool, and the kids are running around, the parents are having beers, and I'm on my phone," he told the group. "One of the other wives comes over to my wife and asks, 'Why is

Mike on the phone all the time?' My wife answers, 'He's on the phone this year so we can come back here next year.'" As Mike finished his story, the group sensed that he told it with a measure of pride. There was some murmuring, some pained looks, and a few comments along the lines of, "Man, that was your vacation with your family." Mike looked a little chagrined and confused as we went to a break.

During the break, one of the other participants pulled me aside and said, "I didn't want to say this in front of the group because I don't want to come across as holier than thou, but I used to work all the time like Mike and now I don't." I asked him how he made the shift and he told me, "I realized one day that I was working like I either already was or was going to be the CEO of this company someday. And then it hit me that I'm not the CEO and really would never even want to be. Once I recognized that, it was actually pretty easy. Don't get me wrong; this company still gets a lot out of me, but the first thing I do every year now is schedule all of my vacation [time]. I don't give it back anymore. And when I'm on vacation, I'm on vacation. I'm not working on vacation."

When this second guy realized that he was living someone else's story, he woke up and made some changes. It's easy, especially when you're living and working in a high-achievement environment, to end up living someone else's story. When he was president and CEO of GE Appliances, Jim Campbell used to see how this dynamic would contribute to the overworked and over-whelmed state that a lot of the young professionals who worked in his organization were living in. In an interview for this book, Campbell shared this observation:

> It gets into lifestyle choices where people, you know, they just overspend. They are living way past what they should be and [it] puts you on that treadmill. . . . If you live within your means, you don't have to worry about what you make; it's

what you spend and that's a whole element that you rarely hear talked about. . . .

I've just seen people do this over the years. You see a 32-year-old person . . . in this big house and driving the BMW . . . putting [himself] on the treadmill. If you get up there, great; but if you don't, you are in for a life of stress.

In fairness to the people Campbell is talking about, it's easy to fall into the story of thinking or feeling like you always need more. It's so common in today's society that researchers have come up with a term for it: *mindless accumulation.*[7] As Tim Kasser notes in his work on the dark side of the American Dream, a big part of society is based on the idea that there is always something else to accumulate.[8] That can be a powerful story, and it takes a lot of mindfulness to recognize and determine whether it's a story that works for you or not.

Get Ready for Your Moment of Truth

How do you become mindful enough to become more aware of your story and perhaps set some different intentions around what comes next? It might entail being ready for and awake to moments of truth when they present themselves and then processing what you learn from them. In working on this book, I have heard and read about many personal moments of truth that have been a turning point for leaders and other high-capacity professionals on the path to the mindfulness alternative.

For instance, in her book *Thrive,* and in her public appearances, media magnate Arianna Huffington tells the story of one of her moments of truth.[9] It was when she woke up in her office in a pool of her own blood after collapsing from exhaustion and hitting her head on her desk on the way down to the floor. By the standard definitions of modern success—power and money—she was among the most successful people on earth. Collapsing in her office was the wake-up call that led to making changes in her life that created a richer and broader definition of what *success* means for her.

Another moment-of-truth example comes from my friend Marilyn. She's a very creative and accomplished learning and development professional in one of the world's largest and most admired companies. She's made a big impact there over the years, but the urgent pace, the bureaucracy, and the internal politics sometimes made her feel like the gerbil on the wheel. Her moment of truth came one afternoon when two of her colleagues asked her to stay in a hotel lobby and watch their purses, briefcases, and suitcases while they made a trip to the business center to finish working on a presentation. Marilyn didn't mind doing that until a false fire alarm went off in the hotel and the noise was incessantly shrieking in her ear. As she told me, "I couldn't leave because I couldn't carry all of those bags with me. I was trapped in the lobby with this head-splitting noise all around me. It was at that point that I knew I needed to make a change." Marilyn still works for the same company but is taking a more relaxed and mindful approach to her work and life. The interesting thing is she's more productive than she's ever been and recently won an award for leading the most innovative project of the year.

The moment of truth for Jeri Finard, CEO of Godiva Chocolatier and former chief marketing officer (CMO) of Kraft Foods, came on her regular New York to Chicago commute. She found herself sitting on the floor at O'Hare Airport in a summer storm in one of her best suits. With her phone plugged into an outlet at floor level, she was desperately trying to make other arrangements to get home to New York to see her daughter in a milestone school event. Although she made it home in time, the absurdity of the whole scene was the moment of truth that told her it was time to make a career change that allowed her to stay closer to home. A few months later she quit her job as Kraft's CMO. The business press couldn't believe that she was leaving her dream job at Kraft, and the speculation was rife about what was really going on. It was as simple as looking for and landing a job that enabled her to reduce her travel from 60 to 80 percent of each month to 20 percent, allowing her to stay closer to home and family. Of course, the sweet perks that come with being the CEO of Godiva aren't bad either.

Maybe you've already had your moment of truth that led to a more mindful approach or maybe it's yet to come. Either way, when it comes, what do you do with it? How do you stay aware and intentional enough to work with it? That's what we'll explore in the chapters to come. Next up: How do you train your body and mind to work with you rather than against you?

Coach's Corner

- What does *mindfulness* mean to you?
- What types of extrinsic interference typically create the intrinsic interference (mental chatter) that keeps you from performing at your best?
- What story do you have about why you're overworked and overwhelmed? Is that a micro story about what's happening lately or a macro story about why you're in this situation in general?
- What other stories could also be true?

---

3 What's Going on in There, and What Can You Do About It?

What You Need to Know About Your Mind-Body Operating System

Keep Breathing, It Just Might Save Your Life

Henry Lescault knew he should have listened to his intuition and passed on this last undercover assignment. But it was too late now. A drug dealer had just threatened to kill him and his family. Henry knew his best response was to keep breathing and keep talking.

What You'll Learn in This Chapter

- The causes of chronic fight or flight
- The impact of chronic fight or flight on your mind and body
- How activating your rest and digest response supports the mindfulness alternative

---

Around four years into his law enforcement career, Henry had already put in his papers to leave his local Massachusetts police department to join the Naval Criminal Investigative Service (NCIS). Henry's specialty was undercover work, and he had a standing rule: Never do undercover work in the town he grew up in. The chances of his cover being blown were just too great. After he had given his notice to leave for the NCIS, though, his bosses pleaded with him to run one last case in his hometown. A drug-dealing ring was breaking into local pharmacies and selling the narcotics they stole to schoolkids. The higher-ups begged Henry to take the case. With the danger to the kids in mind, he reluctantly agreed.

The moment of truth came when Henry, who was not wearing a wire, was supposed to make a buy from a suspect in a park late one night. Henry knew he might be in trouble when he showed up at the appointed time and four guys were waiting for him instead of one. As he was negotiating the purchase, one of the dealers suddenly asked, "Is your name Henry?" Drawing on everything he had learned since studying martial arts as a teenager, Henry silently took a breath, held it briefly, and quietly exhaled. With his life on the line, he calmly replied, "No, it's Dave."

The dealer replied with menace: "Well, you look like a guy named Henry who went to high school with my brother, and that guy is a cop."

Henry's breathing and training took over at that point. "Look," he answered back, "I don't know who you think I am. I don't know your brother. I don't want to know your brother. I am just here to do business."

"You better be," the dealer snarled, "because if you are that guy, I will find your family. I will kill them all, and then I'll come and kill you."

Steady as a rock, Henry said, "You know what, pal, I am a business man. I just want to buy these drugs; here is your money. If you want to cancel the deal, we can cancel it and walk away right now."

Once the money appeared, the deal was done. Henry walked back to the car to radio in the location of the dealers so the bust could be made. (Mobile phones were rare back then.) His radio wasn't working, so he went to a nearby gas station to call in the details using a pay phone. The dealers were arrested, convicted, and put in jail. Henry and his family were safe, and a couple of decades later he told me the story you just read.

What kept Henry alive that night was near perfect synchronicity between his mind and body under conditions of extreme stress. The good news is the same skills, not even nearly as perfectly applied, can help you access the mindfulness alternative to being overworked and overwhelmed. Like they did for Henry, they'll help you live a longer, healthier, and happier life.

What Was Going on Inside Henry and What Goes on Inside You

Our bodies are capable of some pretty amazing things. Many of those things don't even require active intervention on our part. Actually, it's a good thing that they don't. Can you imagine the outcome if you had to actively direct your heart to beat or your lungs to breathe? It wouldn't be pretty, that's for sure.

With some systems in our body, however, it pays for us to mindfully intervene. One of those is the autonomic nervous system (ANS). What Henry did that night in Massachusetts was expertly manage his internal response to a highly threatening external stimulus. What enabled him to do that was his ANS. The ANS along with the central and peripheral nervous systems enables us to do everything we do as human beings. The ANS is subdivided into three complementary systems: the sympathetic nervous system (SNS), the parasympathetic nervous system (PNS), and the enteric nervous system. When you just have "a feeling in your gut," you know the enteric nervous system is at

play, because it's the division of the ANS that controls your gastro-
intestinal function. And although it communicates with the sympathetic and parasympathetic systems, it can operate independently of
either of them.

In the context of this book, we're most concerned with the SNS
and the PNS. Let's take a look at each of them in terms of how they
worked together and separately in relation to how Henry responded
when the drug dealer threatened to go after him and his family. Hope-
fully you'll never face the extreme nature of the threat that Henry faced
that night, but you likely will deal with hundreds of low-grade, often
silent, threats every day that can leave you feeling overworked and
overwhelmed. We can learn a lot about how to deal with those threats
by taking a deeper look at Henry's story.

Fight or Flight

The SNS is where the fight or flight response resides. When the drug
dealer threatened Henry, his fight or flight response was activated.
When Henry saw and heard the threat, a part of his brain called the
thalamus sorted out the details and activated two other parts of his
brain. As you can see in Figure 3.1, one was a relatively small part very
close to the brainstem called the amygdala. The amygdala activated
another part of the brain called the hypothalamus, which signaled
Henry's adrenal glands to release the adrenaline that immediately prepared his body for emergency action. If the danger persisted, his SNS
was on alert to activate other stress-reacting hormones such as cortisol
to keep him revved up after the initial surge of adrenaline diminished.
The other part of the brain that the thalamus connected with when
Henry was threatened was the upper region called the cortex. The cortex, especially the area called the prefrontal cortex (located right behind
your forehead), is where critical and more sophisticated thinking happens.
This is where situations are sorted out and options are developed.

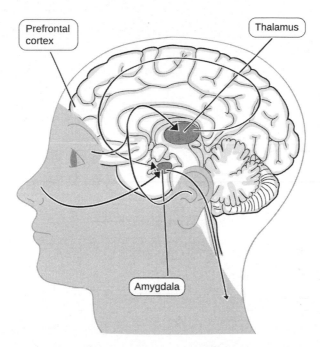

Figure 3.1 How Fight or Flight Starts in Your Brain

Rest and Digest

As Henry quietly took that deep breath when the dealer asked him his name, he began to activate his PNS. The PNS is often called the rest and digest function and, although Henry wasn't doing any resting or digesting at that particular moment, activating his PNS counter-balanced the fight or flight response of his SNS that gave him the space to think through how he wanted to handle a very stressful and danger-ous situation. It also helped mitigate the natural SNS responses of sweaty palms, tight vocal cords, and even crapping in his pants if his digestive system suddenly shut down.

Under your own less dramatic but still stressful circumstances, you want to have the same kind of synchronicity between your SNS and PNS that Henry had in the park that night. It's what scientists and doctors call managing your allostatic load. The goal is to keep your

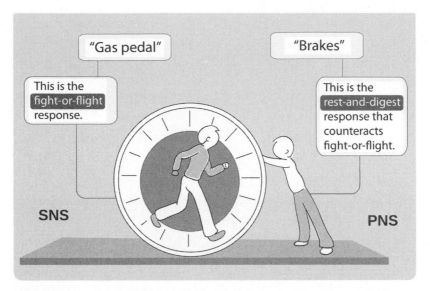

Figure 3.2 Your Gas Pedal and Brakes Need to Work Together

SNS and PNS in a state of balance or homeostasis. Researcher and author Rick Hanson offers a really useful metaphor: The fight or flight (SNS) response is the accelerator, and the rest and digest (PNS) response is the brakes.[1] As Figure 3.2 reminds us, these responses need to work in concert with each other for you to effectively manage your allostatic load.

Stuck in Chronic Fight or Flight

The challenge for many leaders and high-capacity professionals is that the kinds of stress-inducing factors outlined in Chapter 1 can leave them in a low- to high-grade state of chronic fight or flight. In his 30-year law enforcement career, Henry faced his share of life-threatening situations that could trigger an acute fight or flight response. The irony for him, as he told me in our interview, is that his office hours were often more stressful than his time in the field. "The thing about the office stress," he said, "is that it kind of just eats away at you day after day. It's just kind of chinking away at the armor to the point where it will crack." What Henry is describing is the chronic, low-grade state of fight or flight that long-term stress can trigger.

If you've ever paid attention to what you feel like after a 13- or 14-hour day of back-to-back meetings, a hundred or so e-mails, an interminable conference call, dozens of decisions, a contentious conversation or two, and a tough commute, you know what Henry is talking about. Now, add in factors that may or may not be at play in your life, such as business travel, your kids' school and sports commitments, the challenges that come with aging parents or sick loved ones, and financial pressures or worries. If you're also a smartphone-enabled executive, manager, or professional, the likelihood is you never get a true break from any of this on any day of the week. In a study of 1,600 managers and professionals, Harvard Business School professor Leslie Perlow found that:

- 70% check their smartphone within an hour of getting up.
- 56% check their phone within an hour of going to sleep.
- 48% check over the weekend, including Friday and Saturday nights.
- 51% check their phone constantly during vacation.[2]

It's easy to see how all of that stimuli and input can leave you with a fight or flight response that is chronically stuck in the on position.

The impacts of that on your brain and your body are clear.

What Chronic Fight or Flight Does to Your Brain and Body

Let's take the brain first. Perhaps you've noticed that your decision-making capacity isn't at its best when you're feeling chronically stressed. Researchers have demonstrated this in studies. In one study, participants who were placed in conditions that induced chronic stress fell back on habitual strategies (relatively more mindless) even though coming up with new strategies (relatively more mindful) that were directed toward their goals would have been a better way to go. Functional magnetic resonance imaging (MRI) results from the same study showed that chronic stress leads to atrophy of the prefrontal cortex (the part of the brain where higher-order thinking and decision making reside) and in the brain circuitry that controls goal-directed decision making.[3]

So, that's what a chronic state of fight or flight does to your brain. What does it do to your body? Remember that from an evolutionary standpoint, the fight or flight response was what protected our prehistoric ancestors from saber-toothed tigers and other wild beasts that would have been happy to have them for lunch. The threats today—packed calendars, tough decisions, jammed in-boxes, family pressures—are subtler but more persistent. If you end up in a chronic state of fight or flight because of them, the toll on your body can be severe. Because it was designed to address the saber-toothed tiger kind of threat, the fight or flight response amps up systems in your body that you need to respond to danger and amps down bodily systems that aren't required to either fight or flee from the tiger. When those systems get stuck because you're in a state of chronic fight or flight, the effects, which are summarized in Figure 3.3, can be severe and life-threatening.

We're All Psychosomatic

No doubt you've heard the term *psychosomatic illness*. Sometimes it's used in a dismissive way, as in, "Oh, his problems are just psycho-somatic." In other words, "It's all in his head." When you understand the roots of the word—*pyscho* referring to the mind and *somatic* to the

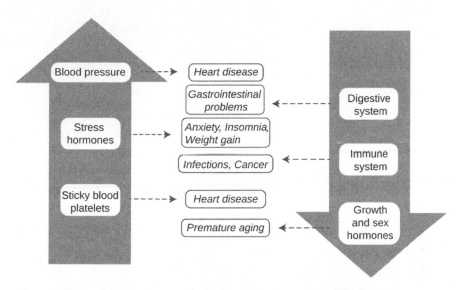

Figure 3.3 The Impact of Being in Chronic Fight or Flight

body—and consider the impact of an ANS that is chronically out of balance, you can see that psychosomatic illness is real and widespread. In fact, as noted earlier, research conducted by the Benson-Henry Institute for Mind-Body Medicine at Massachusetts General Hospital has found that between 60 and 90 percent of all visits to doctors are prompted by stress-induced illnesses.[4] In a 2011 study it conducted of its employees, the health insurer Aetna found that the 20 percent of people who reported the highest amount of stress in their lives had annual medical expenses that were $2,000 higher than average.[5] In the five years that followed the 2008 worldwide financial crisis, a major Greek hospital found that heart attacks among the population of the region it serves leapt 44 percent over the rate from the previous five years.[6]

Statistics like these confirm what Power Yoga creator Bryan Kest said to me in our interview: "The largest factor in our well-being is the place where our mind dwells." Kest's point brings us back to the Tim Gallwey equation about performance that was introduced in

Chapter 2: your performance equals your potential minus the interference. *Performance* refers to both your mind and your body. There will always be extrinsic interference over which you have little or no control. Your well-being and your capacity to overcome overwork and overwhelm depends on the mindfulness of your intrinsic response to the extrinsic stress-inducing interference.

The Promise of Rest and Digest

The entry point to mindfully responding to feeling overworked and overwhelmed is awareness and intention. It's about being aware of the factors that can make you feel overworked and overwhelmed and intentionally activating your rest and digest system to counterbalance your fight or flight system. It's what Dr. Herbert Benson of the Harvard Medical School and a pioneer in mind-body medicine in the West called the relaxation response.

The good news is you can learn to activate your rest and digest system to overcome that overworked and overwhelmed feeling, making it more likely that you show up at your best and generate the kinds of outcomes you hope for at home, at work, and in the community. That's what the mindfulness alternative is all about and what we'll focus on in the rest of this book. We'll work on getting clear on what your unique version of best state performance looks like and identify the simple, practical, easy to apply routines that can help you operate from that best state scenario more often than not.

The additional good news is that by mindfully using your rest and digest system, you can reverse a lot of the damage you may have already done to your brain and body. For instance, one of the routines we'll take an in-depth look at is being aware of and intentional about your breathing. As you may know, taking even a few minutes to intentionally slow down and notice your breathing is one of the foundations of meditation. With the advent of functional MRI machines, all kinds of compelling research is now available that shows the positive impact of mindful breathing and other meditative practices on the structure of the brain.

Research conducted by Eileen Luders and her colleagues at the UCLA Center for Neuroimaging shows that regular meditation increases and thickens (in a good way) the gray matter in the cerebral cortex, which, in turn, improves the brain's capacity for information processing, memory, emotional regulation, and decision making. Perhaps more importantly if you're concerned with minimizing chronic fight or flight, is that regular meditative breathing actually shrinks the size of the amygdala (remember, that's the part of the brain that triggers the fight or flight response).[7]

Meditation is not just good for the brain, it's good for the rest of your body as well. New research suggests that a regular routine of mindful meditative breathing that activates your rest and digest system also make your cells healthier. Your chromosomes have protective caps at their ends called telomeres. Telomeres shorten with age and deteriorate more quickly under conditions of chronic stress.[8] Your body also produces an enzyme called telomerase, which helps extend the useful life of your telomeres. Recent research by a number of scientists, including Nobel Prize winner Elizabeth Blackburn, shows that just 12 minutes a day of meditative breathing can increase telomerase activity by 43 percent. This suggests an improvement in the premature aging caused by being in a chronic fight or flight state.[9]

When I first heard about the positive impact that even a little bit of mindful meditative breathing can have on my mind and body (especially as someone who is serious about managing his multiple sclerosis), I thought, "Why wouldn't I take time every day to mindfully breathe and meditate?" That was a little over a year before I wrote this chapter.

My own bit of anecdotal experience since then is the consistency of taking time daily to sit and breathe for anywhere from 5 to 30 minutes—whatever time I have available—has made a big difference in my energy, stamina, and outlook. If you're looking for a more scientific validation that even a little bit of daily activation of the rest and digest system that can help, consider a recent study from the University of Wisconsin. Stressed-out primary care physicians were given some brief training in mindfulness meditation techniques and encouraged to spend 10 to 20 minutes a day using them.[10] The burned-out doctors reported almost immediate improvements in their stress levels and compassion shown to their patients. By sticking with their simple daily routine, they were holding on to those gains when they reported back a year later.[11]

Easy to Do and Likely to Make a Difference

The findings from studies like these demonstrate that the mindfulness alternative doesn't require you to solve for 100 percent to overcome overwork and overwhelm. As a matter of fact, you shouldn't even try to solve for 100 percent; it's too stressful. Instead, aim for small improvements consistently applied. The kind of small improvements you're looking for are the simple steps that sit in the sweet spot between things that are easy to do and likely to make a difference.

If, through pursuing just a few of the routines that we'll unpack later in this book, you are able to reduce the severity of chronic fight or flight by even 5 percent in a week, that would be a big win. Again, 5 percent may not sound like much, but if you have that 5 percent gain consistently each week, in a month your chronic fight or flight state will be reduced by 20 percent. Keep it up and in three months, you'll have a 60 percent reduction. Now we're talking real impact. As the late UCLA basketball coach John Wooden once said, "When you improve a little each day, eventually big things occur. . . . Seek the small improvement one day at a time. That's the only way it happens and when it happens, it lasts."

Let's now move on to the applied science part of this book. It begins in Part Two with an introduction to your Life GPS®.

Coach's Corner

- What signs, if any, tell you that you might be in a state of chronic fight or flight?

- What are the situations or factors that cause you to go into fight or flight when you're not actually under physical threat?

- What's one easy thing you could do now to activate your rest and digest response? (*Hint:* It involves three deep breaths.) What else could you do?

Part Two

4 Where Do You Want to Go?

Guiding Yourself with a Life GPS

Elaine's Story

In the eight years between writing *The Next Level* and this book, I've coached and spoken to thousands of high-achieving executives, managers, and other professionals. Several hundred of those people have been participants in a 16-person group-coaching program my company offers called Next Level Leadership®. Over the years, I've joked that the next program I'm going to start is a weight-loss program because, more often that not, by the time we get to the last session of Next Level Leadership—seven months after the start, we have one or two participants in each cohort who have lost 25 to 50 pounds.

What You'll Learn in This Chapter

- How a Life GPS can guide you toward the mindfulness alternative

- The components of your Life GPS

- The difference the Life GPS has made for other busy professionals

---

One woman who fits that description is Elaine. On the opening day of the program, she was tense, unhappy with her job, and, like a lot of people who sit in meetings all day long, somewhat overweight. By the time we got to the fifth and final session seven months later, she was almost unrecognizable. Her smiling face was lean, her waist was smaller, and the muscles of her upper arms were well defined. As the group reflected on the changes they'd made over the course of the program, I asked her to share how her own transformation had come about. She told us that the change began just after the second session of the program six months earlier:

> When we were working on the Life GPS in session two, I really started thinking about when in my life I was happiest, felt best, and was at my most productive. I remembered that it was when I swam competitively during high school and college. I always had so much energy and felt so good about life back then. So then I started thinking about the routines I needed to bring into my life to feel that way again. I decided to start swimming again every day like I used to in college.

I asked her how she worked that into a busy schedule at work and home. Her answer was simple: "I quit doing e-mail for the first hour and a half of every morning and went to the pool instead." Then I asked how she dealt with all the e-mails she wasn't responding to first thing in the morning. "Most of them can wait, many of them don't need any reply at all, and I'm more thoughtful and focused about the ones that need my attention," she replied. "The biggest benefit," she went on, "is that I'm so much more focused and productive throughout the day now because of the morning swim. I'm so glad it's back in my life."

By making a simple but significant change in her life, Elaine was pursuing the mindfulness alternative. Although we never even mentioned the word *mindfulness* in that group coaching program, the Life GPS® helped her become mindful. It's a simple tool that can help make a seemingly complex subject like mindfulness more manageable and easier to access. Getting back in the pool was Elaine's path to mindfulness. It had impacts on her life that went far beyond her dress size. It was the best possible way for her to introduce mindfulness in her life (even though she probably would have never thought of it that way), because it was something she was familiar with, loved, and knew how to do. Swimming met her where she was at that point in her life. To make a difference for you, your mindfulness alternative will need to do the same thing for you. The Life GPS is an easy way to organize your mindfulness game plan and to stay on track with it. That's why the rest of this book is organized around the Life GPS framework.

Introducing the Life GPS

As I mentioned in the Introduction, the Life GPS is a personal planning model that my wife, Diane, and I came up with for our own purposes when we were parents of two young boys and had very busy lives filled with work,  family, and community commitments. One of my favorite books at that point in my life was Stephen R. Covey's *The Seven Habits of Highly Effective People.* I probably read it five or six times in those years and had large parts of it practically memorized. Diane loved it too. As much as we drew from it, though, we found its concepts difficult to translate into actions for successfully navigating the challenges of everyday life. The more we thought about it, the more we realized we were basically looking for a "one pager" that would keep us focused on how we wanted to be and the routines that would help us show up in a way that led to the

outcomes that were most important to us in different arenas
of life.

After several months of playing around with different models
and options, we came up with the Life GPS. This was a few years
before the GPS technology that today we're all so familiar with—
and take for granted—became available to consumers. Things were
clearly headed in that direction, but up to that point the GPS had
been reserved for military navigation and other government uses.

Knowing what we knew at the time about the technology,
though, the name Life GPS really appealed to us because the idea
of being intentional about our desired outcomes and having a simple way to keep ourselves focused and on track made a lot of sense
to us. We looked at it as our Life Goals Planning System. Every
November or December we would, and still do, schedule a weekend away for a personal retreat with each other. Honestly, most of
the weekend is reserved for fun and relaxing, but we spend at least
a few hours together reviewing our individual Life GPS sheets
from the current year and talking about what our goals and intentions are for the year to come. A few weeks after the retreat, each
of us finalizes a Life GPS sheet for the next year. We each keep
copies of the current year's Life GPS handy—on our desk, in our
personal planning journals, and, these days, in a PDF on our
iPads, so we can look at them regularly. The only question I ask
myself when I review mine is, "What's one action I need to adjust
this week?" There's usually more than one thing I could adjust,
but I've found over the years that focusing on one thing is easier
and usually has more a meaningful impact than adjusting a lot of
things at once.

After keeping the Life GPS to ourselves for a few years, we started
sharing it with friends; then, when we started the Eblin Group at the
end of 2000, I shared it with selected coaching clients. Since then,
we've shared the Life GPS with thousands of high-achieving

professionals through presentations I've given and through offline and online programs like the one Elaine was in.

One of our early names for what became the Life GPS was the Integrated Life Blueprint. We eventually dropped that name because it just felt like too much of a mouthful, but creating an integrated life blueprint is, in fact, what the Life GPS is all about. It's built around three big questions that, when mindfully considered and acted upon, can change your life. The rest of this book is organized around these questions as a guide to creating the mindfulness alternative to being overworked and overwhelmed. (An example of the Life GPS we provide to our clients is presented as Figure 4.1. If you'd like to download an editable PDF version of the Life GPS for yourself, visit ootma.eblingroup.com.)

How Are You When You're at Your Best?

This first big question, which we'll address in more depth in the next chapter, is all about recognizing the characteristics and behaviors that reflect how you are when you're showing up as the best version of your self. Your answers to that question should be based on the self-knowledge that comes through a bit of quiet reflection on the times in your life when you feel most comfortable and productive. What you're looking for is the non-sports equivalent of what athletes call being in the zone.

The implications of your answers to this question and how they relate to the rest of your life can be surprising and even life altering. For an example of how acting on your best state characteristics can change your life (and the lives of people around you) consider the story of Steve, the founder and president of a successful boutique financial services firm. Steve was a participant in a Life GPS workshop I conducted a number of years ago for a local chapter of the Young Presidents' Organization (YPO). Like most everyone else in YPO, Steve was a

The Life GPS® helps determine your most important goals and sets you on a course to reach them. Get started by clarifying the core characteristics that represent you at your best, the routines that will reinforce peak performance and the outcomes that you hope to create in the three main arenas of life.

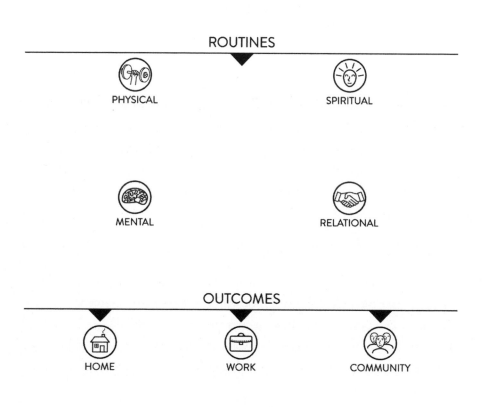

Figure 4.1 The Life GPS Worksheet

driven, ambitious person who was intent on getting results. In the first hour or so of the workshop, he more or less exuded a strong skepticism that any of this stuff about a Life GPS was going to make a damn bit of difference for him. Still, to his credit, he hung in there with the program and agreed to complete a draft of his own Life GPS. When I asked the group to share a bit about what they noticed in the process of completing their one pager, Steve surprised me by acknowledging that he, himself, was surprised.

When I asked him why he was surprised, he shared that one of the characteristics that he believed described him at his best was that he was supportive. "I'm very supportive of my kids and always have been," he said. "Helping them succeed in life has always been important to me. When I was working through the Life GPS, I realized that I had never thought about being intentionally supportive of the people in my company. I've always thought that they're there to do a job, and since I'm paying them to do the job, they should just do it. In the last half hour, I started thinking about what it would look like if I was as supportive of my team members as I am of my kids. It would look a lot different and a lot better, that's for sure."

Steve's story illustrates the value of considering how you are at your best. It gives you a reference point for your best case performance state or your preferred state of being. As you get increasingly clear about that, you begin to see where the leverage is in showing up that way on an integrated basis in all aspects of your life.

What Are the Routines That Would Enable You to Show Up at Your Best?

One of my favorite quotes of all time is from Aristotle: "We are what we repeatedly do. Excellence, then, is not an act but a habit." The basic idea behind this quote is that if you want to be a certain way (excellent, for example), you have to do things that reinforce that state. It's one of those ideas that is so simple it's brilliant.

That's why routines are so important to creating the capacity to consistently show up as the best version of yourself. All of Part Three of this book is dedicated to helping you identify and use the simple and easy to implement routines that, if incorporated into your life, would enable you to show up at your best more consistently and more often. The routines that will become part of your Life GPS fall into four domains:

- *Physical:* Your physical health—energy, strength, flexibility, balance, and stamina—is the foundation for everything you do.

- *Mental:* Your mental acuity and capacity to make mindful choices about your life and work can be enhanced by routines that keep your brain healthy and your neural networks strong.

- *Relational:* The important relationships in your life—with family, friends, coworkers, and loved ones—can be enhanced through mindful routines that keep them vibrant and resilient.

- *Spiritual:* Regular routines can help keep you connected with your answers to the biggest picture question of all—"What am I here on earth to really do?"

Effective routines often have a ripple effect that enables you to show up at your best more often by cutting across one or more of these four domains. For a quick example of how they do this, consider the following note that was sent to me by Tom, a former client who wrote to tell me about the difference the routines he incorporated into his Life GPS have made for him:

> As you may recall, at the time of our coaching program, I was deep in a crisis situation that was consuming my focus almost 24/7. . . . As such, there was little time for anything else, with a stress level that was clearly clouding my judgment and negatively impacting my personal life, as well as my health. During one of the sessions on managing stress, we

discussed how just a small amount of time each day devoted to some type of physical activity could pay huge dividends. While we all know it to be true, it is easy to place exercise at the bottom of the list as I was doing, so I took your words to heart and began running again. The results were almost immediate, and the positive impact this small change had on my well-being and productivity was very meaningful. Now more than two years later, I find time to run every day and no matter the level of stress (oftentimes finding the solution to the problem of the day while pounding the pavement), it always seems more manageable after a good run.

From Tom's note, you can see that he gets a great return on his daily investment in taking the time to go for a run. Clearly, there are physical benefits for him, but there are also mental benefits that enable him to manage his problems and the rest of his life more effectively. To tie things back to the discussion we had about the mind-body operating system in Chapter 3, Tom is mitigating a state of chronic fight or flight by activating his rest and digest response with a daily run. It's likely that his daily running routine has had a positive impact on his relationships and may even give him perspective on what he's really trying to do with his life.

All of that makes the point that you don't need to load yourself up with a bunch of new routines to make it more likely that you show up at your best. The mindfulness alternative relies on choosing a few that are relatively easy for you to do and that are likely to make a difference in your life. More to come on that in Part Three of this book.

What Difference Would Showing Up at Your Best Make in Your Three Big Arenas of Life?

Tom's note hints at the difference showing up at your best can make in the three big arenas of life:

• Your life at *home*

 • Your life at *work*

 • Your life in your broader *community*

Before he renewed and stuck with his running routine, Tom's personal life was suffering along with his work life. As he wrote to me, "the positive impact this small change had on my well-being and productivity was very meaningful."

What difference do you want to make with your life at home, at work, and in your community? In the midst of an overworked and overwhelmed state of life, it can be hard to remember to even ask those questions, let alone answer them. Before we finish the conversation we're having in this book, I hope you'll take time as you read through Part Four to ask and answer them.

You won't be looking for answers that need to last for the rest of your life. Rather, you just want to get clear on the outcomes you're hoping for in each of these arenas as of now. As we discussed at the end of the last chapter, you don't need to solve for 100 percent. That's especially true when trying to define outcomes. So many variables beyond our control are at play in life that spending a lot of time trying to solve for 100 percent just doesn't make much sense for most endeavors. Life is just not that linear. By the time you have enough information to solve for 100 percent, the variables will have changed anyway.

You don't want to get attached to specific outcomes that are not within your span of control, but it's good to have an idea of the quality and nature of the outcomes you want. It's the classic example of the idea that the quality of the journey is as important as the destination. Take your life at home, for example. Almost every parent wants a happy and healthy life for his or her kids. What does that look like exactly? Although there's a lot we can do to create the optimal conditions, there's even more that we can't control. None of that is to say, though, that happy and healthy kids are not a desirable or valid outcome for a parent to strive for in the arena of home. Perhaps the biggest benefit of having that desired outcome is that it informs how you want to show up as a parent who's working for that outcome. That's what I mean about the quality of the journey being as important as the outcome. You have a lot more influence on the former than on the latter.

The same idea applies to your life at work and in your community. Whatever outcomes you determine are important or desirable in those arenas will give you guidance on how you need to show up to make those outcomes possible. That picture of your desired outcomes should also help with the motivation you need to stick with the routines that will help you show up at your best more often than not.

Let's take the next step in creating your mindfulness alternative by considering the first question of the Life GPS—how are you at your best? That's the topic of Chapter 5.

Coach's Corner

- What routines do you have in your life today that help you show up at your best?
- What routines have you had in the past that might help you show up at your best today?
- What difference would consistently showing up at your best make to the outcomes you hope for at work, at home, and in your community?

5 How Are You at Your Best?

Clarifying Your Version of Peak Performance

From Concert to Cellblock

His daughter's school concert was well under way when John Wetzel's smartphone lit up with an urgent text. There was a crisis at the jail where he was the warden. One inmate had taken another hostage. The officers on duty had done everything they could to resolve the situation peacefully, but the hostage-taking inmate was demanding to talk to the warden. Wetzel slipped out of the elementary school audience, got in his car, and headed back to work.

What You'll Learn in This Chapter

- How to identify how you are at your best
- How other accomplished professionals view themselves at their best
- The "uber" factors that can keep you from showing up at your best

---

Thirty-six years old, Wetzel had been the warden for Pennsylvania's Franklin County jail for four years. During that time, he had turned the institution around with a strong emphasis on programs designed to promote a successful reentry into society when inmates left the system. Wetzel's strategy was all about the approaches and treatment that would lead to positive outcomes. As he walked down the main hallway of the jail back to the cells that night, he was thinking to himself, "Shit, man, you build up all this stuff, and here it all goes out the window tonight."

As he approached the cellblock, Wetzel saw that a tactical team was ready to go and that the rest of his staff was looking at him with expressions that were silently seeking his direction. It was at that moment that Wetzel thought to himself, "They are ready to do whatever needs to be done, and they just need to know that I've got it under control."

Wetzel's first words to his staff were, "What's up, boys? Are we going to get this thing done or what?" A young lieutenant on the scene had done a great job of talking to the hostage taker and slowing everything down. As soon as Wetzel looked at the inmate, he could sense that he wanted an out. Wetzel asked him what he was looking for. The inmate answered, "I want respect."

Wetzel replied, "Well, you've got the freaking warden here at 6:30 at night. What else do you want?"

The inmate's shoulders dropped, and Wetzel could see him start to relax. "Are you going to let him out or what?" Wetzel quietly asked.

"Yeah, I'll let him out," the inmate answered.

As the hostage left the area, the warden asked the inmate, "How do you want to do it from here? Do you want me to just cuff you up and take you to the cell, or do you want all of these guys to come in and handle it that way?" Given a choice and a quiet sign of respect, the inmate asked Wetzel to take him back to the cell and the incident was over.

Today, John Wetzel is Secretary of Corrections for the Commonwealth of Pennsylvania and oversees a system with 51,000 inmates, a staff of 15,000, and an annual budget of $2 billion. He is still focused on reforming the prison system and is a national leader in that effort. In a conversation with me for *Overworked and Overwhelmed,* I asked him to talk about the characteristics that describe him when he's operating at his best. Of the close to 50 executives, managers, professionals, and thought leaders I interviewed for this book, he was the only one who began his answer with "A little bit of swagger." The next words on his list were honesty, transparency, and a sense of humor.

Wetzel showed all four of those characteristics the night of the hostage crisis at the Franklin County jail. Your answers to how you are at your best will probably be different than John Wetzel's. What works for him may not work for you. What you have in common with Wetzel, though, is the opportunity to understand how you really are when you're at your best and how to draw on those characteristics to create a reasonable chance of generating the kinds of outcomes you're looking for.

That's what this chapter is about. In the next several pages, we'll talk about why understanding how you are at your best is the foundational platform for the mindfulness alternative. You'll have the opportunity to get clear about how you are at your best and read some insights from other leaders and professionals that might provoke your thinking on your own version of best case performance. Finally, we'll take a look at some of the factors that can get in the way of showing up at your best and how you can set yourself up for success.

Self-Knowledge Is the Beginning of Self-Improvement

Around 2,500 years ago, Socrates taught his students that "the unexamined life is not worth living." A few dozen years later, his intellectual descendant, Aristotle, put a more positive spin on the same idea when he wrote, "Knowing yourself is the beginning of all wisdom." Similarly, in Eastern philosophies, the goal of life is to find, know, and understand your true nature.

Self-knowledge is a journey of a lifetime that is like peeling back the layers of an onion. It's a journey that perhaps never ends but that detail shouldn't dissuade us from starting or taking the journey. The more we understand about ourselves, the more likely we are to live a life that has meaning and makes a difference.

That's why the first of the three big questions in the Life GPS is:

How am I when I'm at my best?

Developing an understanding of how you are at your best becomes a benchmark and reference point for creating the outcomes that are most important in the three big arenas of your life: home, work, and community.

A Spanish proverb says, "Self-knowledge is the beginning of self-improvement," so let's go deeper on the question "How are you when you're at your best?"

Operating at Your Best

When you're operating from how you are at your best, the performance equation $P = p - i$ that we discussed in Chapter 2 transforms from your performance (P) equals your potential (p) minus the interference (i) to simply your $P = p$, performance equals your potential. Operating from how you are at your best is working from a state of pure potential. The interference, whether it's extrinsic ("out there") or intrinsic ("in here") falls away. It's what psychologist Mihaly Csikszentmihalyi has termed *flow*.[1] When you're operating from how you are at your best, you are completely absorbed in what you're doing in the present moment. It's about as close to the exact opposite of being overworked and overwhelmed as you can get.

Think back to the story about John Wetzel and the hostage situation that opened this chapter. Within the few minutes it took to drive back to his jail, Wetzel shifted his attention from being a dad at his daughter's concert to a chief law enforcement officer who had to defuse a potentially dangerous situation. During those few minutes, he thought a bit about everything he had tried to accomplish at the jail to that point and started to worry that all of that effort might be for naught. Then, when he walked into the cellblock, he became totally focused on his role in generating a safe outcome for everyone involved that night. It took the full focus of how Wetzel understands himself to be when he's at his best—a little bit of swagger, transparency, honesty, and a dab of humor to defuse the tension—to convince the inmate that he should peacefully let his hostage go. Wetzel was successful that night because he understood the strengths he was bringing to the situation from his "at his best" case and was fully present when it mattered most.

How to Determine What Your Best Looks Like

So, what does your version of being "at your best" performance look like? Fortunately, you're in the best position of anyone to answer that question. Here's a five-step process for clarifying that in a way that addresses all of the important arenas of your life.

Step 1: Find a Quiet Place

First, find a quiet place where you won't be distracted for 30 or 45 minutes. Perhaps grab a cup of coffee or tea to sip on and find a comfortable seat. Put your feet on the floor or tuck them up under yourself. Close your eyes for a few moments and take three deep breaths.

Step 2: Remember When You Were in the Zone

Now that you're a little more relaxed, consider the past 6 to 12 months of your life. As you do, sketch out a worksheet that looks like the one in Figure 5.1. What peak experiences do you remember from the different arenas of your life—home, work, and community—when you felt completely absorbed in what you were doing, when were you in that state of flow that athletes call being in the zone? On the left hand side of a blank sheet of paper (the tactile nature of writing is a plus for this exercise), start jotting down some headlines that summarize each of those experiences for you. If there

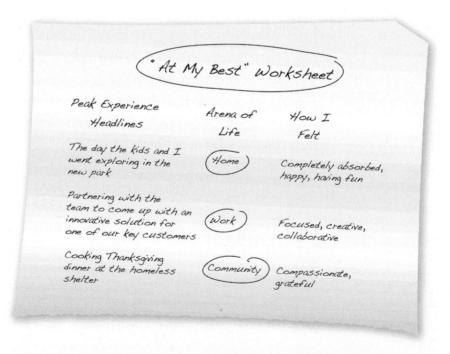

Figure 5.1 Example of an "At My Best" Worksheet

are peak experiences more than a year old that really stand out for you, write down those headlines, too. To the right of each of the headlines, jot down the primary arena for that peak experience—home, work, or community. Your headlines will, of course, be uniquely yours, but examples of what I'm talking about are playing in the park with my kids (home), solving a problem for a key customer (work), and working with a group of volunteers in a local soup kitchen (community). Give yourself at least 15 or 20 minutes to come up with your list of headlines. The first few might come fairly quickly and then you may temporarily run out of ideas. Give yourself a little bit of time and space for other memories to bubble up. Resist the urge to check your smartphone for something interesting if you run out of ideas after the first few minutes. Take a sip or two of your drink and wait for some more peak experience memories to come forth. Write down as many as come to mind.

Step 3: Remember How It Felt

Once you have your list of headlines, use the right side of your worksheet to jot down what it felt like to be in each of those situations. For instance, the headline about playing in the park with the kids might include characteristics like completely absorbed, happy, having fun, and the like. The key customer problem solving scenario might generate descriptors such as calm, creative, focused, or collaborative. The volunteering in the soup kitchen example might remind you of feelings of compassion, gratitude, or perhaps other ways of being focused and absorbed.

Step 4: Look for Common Denominators

Now that you have the list of "at your best" headlines and what each of those moments felt like for you, take three more deep breaths and shift your attention from the dance floor perspective of recalling specific memories about states of performance to the balcony perspective of looking for patterns. What you're doing now is looking for a common denominator among "at your best" characteristics that seem to cut across multiple experiences. Highlight or circle those words. Perhaps you'll need to jot down some other words or phrases that aren't on the page yet but do a good job of summarizing some of the patterns you're seeing. As you're reviewing and massaging your page, watch out for words or ideas that are someone else's view of what your at your best characteristics *should* be. You're not trying to come up with a list of ways that other people think you should be; you're building a list of characteristics that you know from deep personal experience represent you when you're at your best. Of all the "at your best" characteristics that you've identified, which are the ones that resonate with you most deeply? Flag the four to six "at your best" characteristics that stand out the most.

Step 5: Congratulate Yourself

Congratulations, you've just gotten a fix on the short list of characteristics that describe you when you're showing up at your best. If you're creating your Life GPS as you're reading this book, take a few minutes to write your final list under the At Your Best section of the Life GPS worksheet (Again, you can download an editable PDF from ootma.eblingroup.com.)

The Impact of the At Your Best Approach

That list you just created is essentially the true north of your Life GPS. Knowing and understanding how you are at your best gives you a reference point for how you want to show up as a leader, as a professional, as a family member, as a friend, and as a person. What would it look like to apply those characteristics more consistently across the three arenas of life? You'd probably be working against yourself a lot less and end up being a lot more effective.

As shown in Chapter 4's story of Steve, the Young Presidents' Organization member who recognized the opportunity to be as supportive of the people who worked for him as he was for his kids, having a deeper understanding of how you are when at your best can create a lot of positive leverage in your life.

Barbara's Story

Another example of how this works comes from Barbara, a senior director in a large bank who was a participant in a *Becoming a Mindful Leader* workshop I led. She shared with us that she used to think that she needed to be one type of person at work and another type of person outside of work. She explained that the work version of herself had historically been a tough, no BS, suck it up and do your job kind of persona. That's what she thought she had to do to succeed. Meanwhile, her non-work self was fun, loving, and joyful with family and friends. She found the constant shifting between these two versions of herself to be exhausting and demoralizing. One day she decided to just be the family and friends version of herself all the time, including at work, and let the chips fall where they may. To her surprise and delight, she's been more successful and happier at work since she recognized and made the shift. What she really wanted was to just be her true self all the time. Awareness of how she really is at her best and a simple shift in her actions helped her do that.

Diane's Story

Yet another example comes from my wife, Diane. When we were young parents to our two boys, Andy and Brad, we faced the usual stresses that most parents face. Unfortunately, that can manifest itself in yelling at the kids when things don't go the way you want. One day, one of the boys had a friend over to play and the friend did something that violated one of our house rules. Rather than yelling at the kid, Diane quietly asked him to stop doing what he was doing and explained why we didn't do that in our house. The little friend stopped and went about his business. It was at that moment that Diane asked herself, "Why am I nicer to my kid's friends than I am my own kids?" From that point on she resolved to always have a conversation with our boys rather than a shouting match. Diane recognized that at her best, she was calm, warm, and deliberate. Showing up that way with everyone, including our kids, became a goal for both of us. Was it a perfect record from there on? Heck, no (especially for me), but it made a big difference. What did we both really want? A strong and loving relationship with our sons throughout their lives. Now that they're 25 and 21 years old, the report is so far, so good. Awareness and a simple shift in our actions (led by Diane) helped us get that.

"What If I'm Stuck?"

If you've never stopped to consider how you are at your best, it can be tough to come up with your first pass of the characteristics that describe you when you're operating at your best. To give you an idea of how other leaders and professionals have answered the question, I've put together this table that summarizes the answers of a little less than half the people I've interviewed for *Overworked and Overwhelmed*. As you review their responses, give some attention to the similarities and differences that cut across the different people. Let's compare notes on the other side.

Name	Role	"At My Best" Characteristics
Adam Grant	Wharton professor, author of *Give and Take*	Completely absorbed, flow, helping someone else in a meaningful way, elevated

Name	Role	"At My Best" Characteristics
Andy Ajello	Senior Vice President, Novo Nordisk	Calm but still full of energy, steady, crisp
Caralyn Brace	Vice President and General Manager, Unisys	Confident, clear, intentional, honest, genuine, calming to others
Caroline Starner	Senior Vice President, Oakley	Calm, clear, confident, intentional
Crystal Cooper	Vice President, Unisys	Relaxed, approachable, comfortable, prepared, confident
Chris Nassetta	Chief Executive Officer, Hilton Worldwide	Aware, present
Danae Ringelmann	Cofounder and Chief Customer Officer, Indiegogo	At ease, comfortable, happy with my strengths, not stressed about weaknesses or gaps
Elizabeth Bolgiano	Chief Human Resources Officer, AMAG Pharmaceuticals	Reflective and purposeful before acting
Henry Lescault	Former Federal Agent	Connected with people, confident, centered, laserlike focus
Jim Campbell	Former Chief Executive Officer, GE Appliances	Positive, sending the right signals, bringing the pieces of the plan together
John Rawlinson	Actor, model, founder, Integrated Wellbeing	Staying present with my responses, responding authentically, feeling the emotion, being with it and responding calmly

(continued)

(*continued*)

Name	Role	"At My Best" Characteristics
Kaye Foster Cheek	Former Chief Human Resources Officer, Johnson & Johnson and Onyx Pharmaceuticals	Open, vulnerable, fearless, truly loving (as the opposite of fear), strong, rooted
Lynn Pendergrass	Worldwide Chairman, Consumer Segment, Johnson & Johnson	Sharp, energetic, focused, happy, thoughtful, deliberate, true to myself, looking at the bigger picture
Melissa McLean Jory	Nutritionist and exercise scientist	Calm with energy, productive, focused, at my own pace
Monica Oswald	Vice President, financial services company	Calm, happy, joyful
Paul Hiltz	Chief Executive Officer, Community Mercy Health Partners	Grateful, listening, asking questions, connected, a little bit slower, not rushing through things
Per Wingerup	Vice President, Learning and International HR, CBS Corporation	In flow, creative, at peace, in harmony with myself, my thoughts, and my surroundings; very focused on the task at hand
Ron Shaich	Chief Executive Officer, Panera Bread	When I'm searching, having empathy for others, being in an open, searching place, feeling internal peace, I'm doing what I respect
Susan Piver	Author and founder, Open Heart Project	My mind is sharper, my heart is calmer

What did you notice about the responses of these 19 people? What's similar, and what's different? There are a few things that strike me about the words that these leaders and professionals think of to describe themselves at their best. First, some of them, such as Caroline Starner of Oakley and Elizabeth Bolgiano of AMAG Pharmaceuticals, are very concise and specific with their lists. Others, such as Adam Grant of Wharton and Ron Shaich of Panera Bread, are a bit more conceptual and expansive in how they describe it for themselves. From my perspective and experience of working with clients on their Life GPS, either approach is great as long as it works for you.

Another thing that I notice from the list is how often some of the same words or ideas come up for multiple people. Words such as *calm*, *confident*, and *focused* come up a lot. Some of the "at my best" lists are more focused on results while others lean more toward relationships. Some of the lists strike a balance between the two. The similarities and differences among the responses show that there is no right answer to the question "How are you at your best?" The right answer is your answer. The interesting thing is that your answers to "How are you at your best?" may change over the years. That's cool. If you stick with this process year over year, your answers probably will change. That's called accumulating wisdom through gathering life experience, reflecting on it, and learning from it. For now, though, start where you are. Your answers to the question are the right answers for you right now.

What Gets in the Way of Showing Up at Your Best

So, when you read the title of this section, I wouldn't be surprised if your response was something along the lines of "What gets in the way of me showing up ay my best? How long have you got!?" Yeah, I know there's a lot of stuff going on out there. That's all of that extrinsic interference we've been talking about that makes you feel so overworked and overwhelmed. There are things you can do to mitigate some of that (we'll get to them in the next chapter), but there's always going to be a lot of extrinsic interference that you can't control. The mindfulness alternative to being overworked and overwhelmed focuses on your intrinsic response to all of that extrinsic interference. Just as a reminder, the goal is to get you out of chronic fight or flight syndrome by mindfully activating your rest and digest system. Doing so will give you the physical and mental resources to more effectively respond to all of the extrinsic interference that, if not effectively addressed, can peg your fight or flight RPM in the red zone and leave you feeling depleted, exhausted, burned out, and hopeless (pick your favorite word).

Part Three of this book will help you identify the mindful routines— physical, mental, relational, and spiritual—that will support keeping your rest and digest response in play and enable you to show up at your best more often. For now, though, let's take a quick look at three "uber" factors that can get in the way of showing up at your best.

Uber Factor 1: Kinks in the Hose

The first uber factor is what my friend Dinabandhu Sarley calls the kinks in the hose. Having served as the CEO of the Kripalu Center for Yoga & Health, as the president of the Omega Institute, and for 20 years as a yoga monastic, in addition to having taught thousands of hours of yoga and wellness classes, Dinabandhu is not exactly the poster boy for being overworked and overwhelmed. He's actually very busy with a life full of commitments, but he's not overcome with all of it. He's definitely worth listening to.

One of the big ideas in the yoga tradition is *prana*. It's a Sanskrit word that translates as "life force." The idea is that prana is the universal energy that runs through the human body. If it is able to flow freely and unimpeded through the body, then you show up at your best and good things happen. When the prana doesn't flow freely, it's like there's a kink in the hose. Just like the water doesn't flow when there's a kink in your garden hose, the prana doesn't flow when you create kinks in the metaphorical hose. (By the way, if you're getting hung up on the word *prana*, try *mojo* instead. The idea is much the same.) The larger point is that your energy and potential are being blocked by the intrinsic interference that comes up in your mind when the extrinsic interference overwhelms you. That's what keeps you from showing up at your best or being in the zone.

So, how do you get the kinks out of the hose? First, understand that the kinks are caused by the anxiety that comes from focusing on all the extrinsic interference that you can't control. Next, understand that a good bit of that interference might actually be your brain playing some tricks on you. As Rick Hanson summarizes in an article for *Psychology Today* why that's the case:

> The alarm bell of your brain—the amygdala (you've got two of these little almond-shaped regions, one on either side of your head)—uses about two-thirds of its neurons to look for bad news: it's primed to go negative. Once it sounds the alarm, negative events and experiences get quickly stored in memory—in contrast to positive events and experiences, which usually need to be held in awareness for a dozen or more seconds to transfer from short-term memory buffers to long-term storage.[2]

How do you deal with negativity bias? Basically, you need to name it and claim it. Recognize the bias as that little voice in your head that sends you into that downward spiral of negativity and stress. You know what it sounds like:

> Wow, this sucks. I'll never get through all of this. I don't even know where to start. How did I get myself into this situation? Why do I always do that to myself? Am I just stupid or what? I shouldn't even be in this job. They either made a mistake hiring me or I made a mistake taking it. I wish I could quit. But I can't quit because I have a mortgage and three kids to put through college.

Okay, you get the idea. Those are the kinds of internal monologues that put kinks in your hose. We all have them from time to
time, but they're easier to avoid or stop in their tracks when you're
aware that you're having them. These kinds of negative monologues
are what Richard Carlson and Joseph Bailey called thought attacks in
their book, *Slowing Down to the Speed of Life*.[3] Having a name for the
process can help you recognize when it's occurring and take steps to
mitigate it. My favorite name for it is the itty-bitty shitty committee.
We'll talk more about how to minimize the impact of the itty-bitty
committee in the upcoming chapter on mental routines.

Uber Factor 2: Too Much of a Good Thing

The second uber factor that can get in the way of showing up at your
best is the too much of a good thing scenario. In my primary field of
leadership coaching, it's a well-known fact that your strengths, when
overused, can become your weaknesses. As much as you want to rely
on the strengths that flow from you being at your best, you can't do it
all. It's important (for lots of reasons) to give other people the opportunity to play from the strengths that flow from *their* being at *their*
best. It's what I referred to in *The Next Level* as picking up team reli-
ance and letting go of self-reliance. (By *team,* I mean both formal and
informal. Your team could be the people you work with or the people
you live with.) In any case, you want to create opportunities for others
to contribute so that you can operate from your sweet spot and they
can operate from theirs.

Back in Chapter 2, we learned a lot about mindfulness from
former U.S. Coast Guard Commandant, Admiral Thad Allen. In a
conversation for this book, he shared with me how he keeps track of
everything that demands his attention during a crisis situation like
Hurricane Katrina or the Deepwater Horizon oil spill. Although
Allen is an outstanding strategic thinker himself, the demands of

crisis situations require that he pay a lot of attention to what's happening right now as opposed to what might happen down the road. Still, the long-term possibilities are important, so what does Allen do about that? As he told me, "I outsource it." He always designates two or three of his team members in a crisis situation to pay attention to what's going on around the edges and what's developing on the horizon. They analyze and distill all of that information and bring back to him what they think he needs to be aware of or act on. Could Allen do that function himself? Sure, if he didn't have anything else to pay attention to. You might be able to do everything, but it's pretty certain you can't do everything at once. Allen recognizes that and makes sure he operates at his best by enrolling and allowing others to operate from their best.

Uber Factor 3: Playing Against Your Strengths

The third uber factor that can get in the way of your showing up at your best is working too hard to be good at stuff that you're just not wired to be good at. It's easy to get caught in the trap of thinking, "Unless I learn how to do this, I won't be a full-fledged leader, professional, human being, or whatever." I'm not saying that you shouldn't learn how to do new things that might be challenging at first. That's one way we grow. All I'm saying is show some discernment about the things you devote your time and attention to mastering. Otherwise, you're just going to keep putting kinks in the hose that keep your best state characteristics from flowing through.

Danae Ringelmann, the founder and chief customer officer of the crowdfunding website Indiegogo learned this lesson along the way. After months and years of working against it, Ringelmann told me:

> [I] finally embraced the fact that I'm not organized. I'm not an organized person. I was reading books on how to be more

organized and asking people what their organization systems are and how they do all the e-mail and all that kind of stuff.

It's like it's just not who I am, so it's not just what can I do to accept that, but what other system can we put in place that accepts that, and then manages the impact of me not being organized.

Ringelmann is a very accomplished person who's on *Fortune* magazine's list of the 40 most influential people under age 40. She gets stuff done in a big way, but being super organized is not on the list of how she is at her best. The cool thing is she's recognized and accepted that and figured out ways to work with it. That allows her to put more energy and focus into actually showing up at her best.

And that, in the end, is perhaps what Socrates had in mind when he said, "My friend . . . care for your psyche . . . know thyself, for once we know ourselves, we may learn how to care for ourselves." That's the approach that's going to enable you to show up as how you are at your best and reduce the overwork and overwhelm.

There is, though, one commitment you have to make if any of this is going to work for you. We'll explore what that commitment is and how to follow through on it in the next chapter.

Coach's Corner

- What does it mean to you to be in the zone or in flow?
- When was the last time you felt that way?
- What were the conditions that made it feel that way?
- What characteristics describe you when you're at your best?

6 What's Their Secret?

The One Commitment You Have to Make to Yourself and How to Keep It

Learning to Clear the Decks

Like almost everyone else who ends up in a big job, Caroline Starner, Oakley's global senior vice president of human resources, worked her way up through jobs where she learned her craft. Sometimes in those roles you end up in situations where you feel like you're in way over your head. That happened to Starner early in her career, and it shaped the way she's approached her life and work ever since.

What You'll Learn in This Chapter

- The one commitment you need to make to successfully pursue the mindfulness alternative
- Where responsibility for that commitment lies
- Ten tips for keeping that commitment

Starner shared her story with me:

I was fresh out of college, and I had an important role running a
department within a function. I was feeling completely overwhelmed. I just could not see how to get all the tasks done. So I
made a list of all the things that had to happen as evidence of how
tremendously overwhelming and how impossible it was going to
be to accomplish all this. Then I sort of started stalking my boss
to show him that I can't get all this stuff done.

Needless to say, Starner's boss wasn't leaping at the opportunity to
sit down with her, wave his magic wand, and solve all of her problems.
She was persistent, though, and with some exasperation, he agreed to
take a look at her list.

There were two things he said to me that have stuck with me forever. One is "Don't bring me problems; bring me solutions." The
second is when I actually got him to sit down to look at my list, he
ticked through everything on it and took it apart. He was like,
"Look, if you need to get this done, you can get a temp. If you
need to get this done, why does this have to happen this week?
Do that next week." He kind of methodically went down the list
and moved it out so that it all got done but in a different way. I left
the meeting feeling a little silly actually because I was like, "Wow,
okay. That makes a lot of sense." So that's what I practice now
pretty much on a regular basis.

Starner's boss helped her solve her short-term sense of overwork
and overwhelm that day and, in the process, taught her an important
lesson that has helped her effectively manage her career and life since
then. It's analogous to the proverb that if you give someone a fish, he
eats for a day; if you teach him to fish, he eats for a lifetime. What
Starner learned that day was that the only person who was going to
keep her from feeling overworked and overwhelmed was her. Since
then, she's been practicing the one commitment that every successful
leader and high-capacity professional I've worked with or talked to has
made to themselves. *That commitment is to intentionally manage their
time so they have a fighting chance of showing up at their best. That's their*

secret. If you want to move beyond being overworked and overwhelmed, you've got to do the same thing.

Ten Tips That Can Help You Keep That Commitment

Part Three of this book will help you identify routines in the physical, mental, relational, and spiritual domains that will help you show up at your mindful best. Managing your time effectively is the commitment you have to make to create the space for the routines that will make the mindfulness alternative possible. This chapter will help you do that by flagging 10 best practice time management tips that I've identified in conversations with or observations of high-capacity people. The good news is you don't have to adopt all 10 tips to make a positive difference against feeling overworked and overwhelmed. In fact, I'd discourage it, especially if you're considering adopting all 10 tips at once. That's just a recipe for feeling more overwhelmed. Instead, review what others have learned and start with the one or two best practice time management tips that would be relatively easy for you to do and likely to make a difference in honoring your commitment to effectively manage your time. Remember, when it comes to carving out the time you need for the mindfulness alternative, the only person who's going to take care of you is you.

Time Tip 1: Recognize and Overcome the Tyranny of the Present

Even though the subtitle of this book is *The Mindfulness Alternative,* no one is suggesting that all you focus on is what's happening right this second. As Adam Grant, Wharton professor and author of *Give and Take,* said to me, "Sometimes I get the impression that when people talk about mindfulness, they think you should be in the moment all the time. I think there's nothing more dangerous. People who are (always) in the moment never actually pick up their heads and look ahead and make plans and pursue goals and dreams."

Caroline Starner offered additional perspective on this point when she observed:

> I've heard people say, "Mindfulness is about being in the present." Okay, it's about being in the present, but you can't just be in the present and ignore what you have to accomplish and what steps you're going to take to get to the future.
>
> So, to me, mindfulness is just the focused understanding of what you need to do . . . managing the various aspects of your life in a calm, thoughtful fashion and [asking], "Okay, what has to happen today versus tomorrow?"

If you're spending your days reacting to and dealing with what's right in front of you, you're likely succumbing to what former U.S. Coast Guard Commandant Thad Allen refers to as the "tyranny of the present." Since a good part of Allen's career was spent in the gerbil wheel known as Washington, D.C., his version of the tyranny of the present included "incessant data calls from the Hill," budget battles, spur of the moment meetings with Cabinet secretaries, and meetings at the White House. Although the specifics of your gerbil wheel may be different, you can likely relate to Allen's observation that "You could . . . work 12 hours a day and go home (having been) completely responsive to everything anybody asked you to do and gotten nothing done."

Allen's mental model for overcoming this was to think of his work as a poker game and all of the demands that made up the tyranny of the present as the ante for staying in the game. They were the table stakes. His goal was to "make that as effective and efficient as possible" to minimize the amount that has to be put on the table to start the game. "You want to minimize the ante, but you've got to stay in the game." There's a certain amount of stuff you've got to do every day to keep the game going, but keeping your ante of that stuff as low as possible gives you the space to actually be fully present for the things that matter most.

Time Tip 2: Ask, "Is This Really Even Necessary?"

One way to keep your table stakes low is to regularly ask yourself, "Is this really even necessary?" Think about the meetings you go to on a regular basis, the conference calls you dial into, the reports you write or read. When was the last time you questioned the assumptions or needs underlying any of that? Chances are, you're doing things on a regular basis that aren't really even necessary. How many hours a week does that unnecessary work add up to? The answer might surprise you. In more than 50 years of consulting to organizations around the world, Peter Block has seen his share of wasted time. In an interview for this book he bet that of the 72 hours a week the typical overworked and overwhelmed professional is clocking on work, 40 of those hours are spent doing unnecessary things. Does 40 hours a week of unnecessary work sound unrealistically high to you? Maybe it is, but isn't it worth asking the question? Even if you could recapture five hours a week by regularly asking, "Is this really necessary?" wouldn't that be a pretty big win? Think about what you could do with an extra five hours a week. In our conversation, Peter encouraged me to ask you to "confront how much of the work that (you're) doing isn't necessary, even though it's the norm." (Mission accomplished, Peter.)

Asking this question might require you to suspend the belief that everything you do is critical. As Kaye Foster Cheek, the former head of human resources for Johnson & Johnson, said to me, "You've got to challenge the underlying assumption that more is better and . . . really start to get comfortable with the fact that doing one less thing might actually make you more effective."

Time Tip 3: Push Your Calendar's Reset Button

Sometimes the answer to "Is this really even necessary?" will be, "Yes, but not right now." As Caroline Starner noted in my interview with her, "There can be 10,000 things coming at you in the workplace, and you're not going to get 10,000 things done in a day. So what's most important to get done today? To set you up for tomorrow? What could be postponed? What could be outsourced? What could be done by someone else? What should not just be done at all?"

In the years since her first boss sorted through her to-do list and told her to reschedule most of what was on it, Starner has become a master of regularly pushing the reset button on her calendar. Her cue for doing that is when she starts to feel distracted or interrupted by issues that don't match up with her priorities. When this happens, she resets or clears her calendar as much as possible to create space for the initiatives that matter most. Her goal is to "reorganize the things that still have to get done. You can't just ignore them; you just can't not do them. But it's a refocusing, and it's a scheduling of those distractions to a future time."

Time Tip 4: Understand and Set Your Operating Rhythm

Just about every high-performing leader and professional I've worked with or interviewed has established a set of life routines that, collectively, comprise his or her personal operating rhythm. Through experience and self-observation, these individuals have learned what works for them in optimizing their time, energy, and attention throughout the day. It's what Thad Allen calls "normalizing the context. . . . Once you do that, then everything else becomes a variation on a theme."

The operating rhythm for most of the high-capacity professionals I've talked with usually begins early in the day. On the days when he was working in Washington, D.C., Allen's operating rhythm started with a 15-mile bike ride to work at 6:00 AM. In addition to providing some exercise, the 45-minute ride was his time to think, plan, reflect, or just let his mind wander. Once he got to the office, he grabbed a cup of coffee and cooled down while checking his e-mail. Then he took a shower, got dressed, and reviewed his schedule for the rest of the day. From there, he was off and running.

In his job as vice president of learning and international human resources for CBS Corporation, Per Wingerup has come up with an operating rhythm that accommodates his frequent business travel while providing the consistency he needs to perform at his best. He's learned that he's not a first thing in the morning exerciser, so when he gets up around 5:30 in the morning, the first hour or so is spent on reading and doing some stretching in his room. Wingerup is energized by being outside, so he always tries to walk to the office around 7:00 in the morning and will stop by a Starbucks for a coffee and a breakfast bite on the way. He's learned that the best thing for him in the first hour of work is to stay off e-mail and do some reading that feeds his creative side. He's usually very dialed in to his work between 8:00 and 10:30 AM. If he doesn't have calls scheduled before lunch, he'll head to the gym for an hour because its usually empty then and he can be really efficient with his work-out. After a shower and grabbing a bite to eat, he's back in his office by noon. The next four hours are almost always productive ones for him. If he has meetings, he tries to schedule as many as possible around a walk or a trip to Starbucks. Movement keeps him energized. Wingerup has noticed over the years that his attention to detail dips after 4:00 PM so he spends the last few hours of the day on big-picture creative work and stays away from writing reports or anything that requires heavy duty math.

As president and CEO of Hilton Worldwide, Chris Nassetta regularly clocks long days across multiple time zones. His job requires frequent travel to Hilton properties and projects around the world, as well as multiple meetings a day with colleagues, customers, investors, the media, community leaders, and the like. The most important part of his operating rhythm is taking time early in the day to prepare. Here's what he told me the first few hours of a typical day are like for him:

> I get up naturally early at around 5 AM. Then I generally do my e-mails. I am at the office by 6 AM., and generally very few people are there. I get myself organized for the day so I can be present later and minimize distractions. Then when I start my day dealing with people at around 7:30 AM to 8:30 AM, I have already gotten organized in my mind.
>
> I know what I need to do for the day. I know what is most important. I know there will be interruptions, but I have read what I need to read to be prepared and am ahead of the game. So when I am dealing with somebody it's a lot easier to be focused on them instead of thinking, "Oh no, I have to give a speech this afternoon."
>
> I compartmentalize it. I pull that file out of my head when I need it, but I am prepared.

Because Crystal Cooper's work as Unisys's vice president of public sector for North America is very customer facing, her operating rhythm requires a lot of flexibility. Her team members and partners are located all over the United States and around the world, so she has a lot of conference calls and travel that span time zones. Since she's based on the West Coast that can make for some pretty early mornings on the phone. Twelve-hour days are typical for Cooper, and proposal team meetings or customer dinners can regularly make her days even longer. Like that of Wingerup, Nassetta, and so many professionals today, Cooper's business operates in a global, 24/7 environment. Here is what Cooper thinks about that and the decisions she's made about managing her operating rhythm under demanding conditions:

I think that a lot of people are angry that the world is 24/7. I just had to get past that and stop fighting against that and acknowledge that that's what it is. As soon as I did that, it was easier for me to incorporate those activities that I needed in order to take care of myself and my family and get the job done that I needed to get done. . . . Trying to keep it within what that typical day might be is not always reality. . . . What I have found is I'm getting better at just carving out time during that 24-hour period to take care of myself and those other needs. It just doesn't stick within a set period of time any longer given the globalization and the 24-hour, seven-days-a-week nature that the world has evolved to.

As Cooper's comments suggest, even the best laid plans of sticking with an operating rhythm can change depending on extrinsic circumstances. It might have been summed up best in one of my favorite quotes of all time from the well-known boxer and philosopher Mike Tyson: "Everybody has as a plan until they get hit." When external factors disrupt your day, it's important to accept it and roll with it so you can get back on track more quickly. What Carl Jung wrote is true: "What you resist, persists." As Tracy Columbus, a longtime personal manager for actors and other artists, said to me, "There is a recognition . . . that some days you sell and some days life happens, and it's better to just sit and create, or bead or go through a Southwest art magazine for 20 minutes and replenish. I think that's okay because it's when we are overworked and overwhelmed that things become very rote and that's when the grayness takes over life's palette."

Time Tip 5: Schedule the Most Important Rocks First

You've probably heard the story about the physics professor who had a large glass jar on his lab table surrounded by some big rocks, a beach pail full of pebbles, and a smaller jar full of sand. He asked his students if all of that would fit in the big jar. The consensus was no. Then the professor proved them wrong by putting the big rocks in first, pouring the pebbles in to fill the gaps between the rocks, and then adding the sand to fill in the space between the pebbles. His point, of course, was if you want to fit everything in, the big rocks have to go in first. (In my favorite version of the story, after the sand goes in and the jar is filled to the brim, he asks if anything else could possibly go in. In response to a chorus of no's, he reaches under his table and pulls out a can of Budweiser. He cracks the can open and slowly pours its contents into the jar while reminding the students, "You always need to leave time for a beer.")

Scheduling their most important rocks first is a common theme I've heard from and observed in high-capacity professionals. They're clear about what else is important to them other than work and make sure that those items go on their calendars first. It could be regular time with family and friends, exercise, vacations, community work, or hobbies that help them relax. Those kinds of important rocks get on their calendar first.

For Chris Nassetta of Hilton, it's a standing Tuesday night dinner with his dad. As he shared with me:

> My dad and I have been having dinner every Tuesday night since I was 10 years old. My dad is 83, going on 84. I am 51, going on 52, so we have been doing it for 40-plus years.
>
> Now when I am out of town or he is out of town, we don't do it, but I try my best to be around on Tuesdays and we bring lots of guests. Father John and others are going to be there tomorrow. We invite all sorts of interesting people. My kids come, my wife comes, my brothers come, my brothers-in-law come. . . . It's one of those things that I rely on.

As Nassetta said, there are some Tuesdays where dinner with his dad doesn't happen, but there are a lot that do because he schedules them. His approach was echoed to me by Jim Campbell, the former CEO of GE Appliances:

> The best tip I can give people is use your calendar. . . . You have to block the time off and you've just got to build it into your calendar. . . . There are always things that will happen from time to time, but if you don't build it into your weekly and monthly schedules, that's when you don't get things done.

This tip really depends on being clear about what your most important rocks are and scheduling from there. Evolent Health CEO Frank Williams described the process in a pretty compelling way for me:

> If you and I were to sit down and say, "Look, what are the three most important priorities that exist in your life?" and then I list those out, let's just say that exercise is one of them. Then I say, "Well, wait a minute—am I doing that every day?" Then the answer is "no." I think it becomes a real question of "Why?" Why don't I flip the pyramid and say, "Look, if those are the three most important priorities, then those get scheduled first and everything else gets scheduled after."

The more systematic you can be in scheduling your big rocks first, the better. In a 2013 interview with *McKinsey Quarterly,* Ford Motor Company CEO Alan Mulally described the process that worked for him and his family when his kids still lived at home:

> You first have to ask, "What gives me energy?" There can be lots of sources: your family, exercise, your spiritual well-being. Try to combine those, along with your work demands, into one integrated calendar so that everything is built into your lifestyle. You can get beyond having to tell yourself, "Okay, I'm going to have my family life next year in August, on vacation." Instead, jot down what is really important to you, see if you have allocated time for it, and adjust the calendar if necessary. In our house, we had a family meeting every week—the family BPR (business plan review)—where we reviewed what we needed to do and the support required to get us through the week. It is another kind of process step, and a really important one.[1]

Time Tip 6: Give Yourself Time for Unconscious Thought

You've probably noticed a theme in the stories we've heard so far from different high-capacity professionals— they're deliberate about giving themselves some time for unstructured or unconscious thought. What is unconscious thought anyway? You may be thinking, "Isn't it conscious by definition?" Not really. As researcher Loran Nordgren explained in the Autumn 2013 issue of *Strategy and Business,* unconscious thought is the more intuitive, right-brain kind of thinking that leads to flashes of insight about how to solve problems.[2] If you're one of those people who've noticed that you get some of your best ideas while you're in the shower or doing yard work, you know what Nordgren is talking about.

Giving yourself time for unconscious thought is a key component of making effective decisions when there is a large amount of data or a complex problem to solve. The research of Nordgren and his colleagues shows that people make their best complex decisions when they have an opportunity to review the data or the facts and then focus their attention on something else for a while. It's a process of what Richard Carlson and Joseph Bailey called putting a problem on the "mental back burner" to simmer awhile.[3]

Deferring an important decision until you have had a chance to let it simmer is not only proven to be more effective in reaching good outcomes but also lessens your sense of being overworked and over-whelmed. Give yourself time for unconscious thought. That may look a lot like taking a walk, riding your bike, cleaning your house, or playing with your kids.

It might also look like structuring time into your day or week to get away from your normal workflow and work environment. That's what works for Brian Halligan, the CEO of the web marketing firm HubSpot. Haligan makes a distinction between professionals being managers and makers. In his role as CEO, most of his time is spent as a manager—sitting in meetings, reviewing budgets and presentations, answering e-mails, and making calls. Those are mainly conscious thought activities. It's also important for him, though, to spend time as a maker—considering new strategies, products, or trends in the market; crafting a new presentation; and engaging in other more complex creative pursuits that require some unconscious thinking. To make sure he gets that kind of time, Halligan works from home on Wednesdays. When I asked him in an interview how he decided on this plan, he answered:

> It's a break in the middle of the week is all. Nothing great. It's not like some brilliant thing. It's the middle of the week. I'm also an introvert, and so I just need some time away from humans. . . . When I'm working at home, alone with my dog, I lose track of time. I just completely lose track of time. . . . Two or three hours will go by and I'm like, "Wow, I just ran through a bunch of stuff." I just try to get more time to think and less time staying in meetings hearing all the input.

Even if you can't work from home one day a week, you can likely find some time during the week to slip out of the building or to a conference room on another floor for some nonconnected time to do some unconscious thinking. It's important enough to make it one of those big rocks you schedule first.

Time Tip 7: Set Boundaries and Guardrails

Do you remember the first story I shared in the Introduction? It was the one about the room full of 80 or so high-potential corporate managers who were venting heartily about the impossible pace of meetings, travel, and e-mails they were expected to keep at all hours of the day and night. All of them were ranting except for Susan, the woman who told the group that she had made a decision years before that unless there was a true emergency (and they were rare), she was leaving at 6:00 PM each evening to go have dinner with her family. And, although she would take urgent and important business calls at home, she didn't spend the evening on her smartphone answering e-mails either.

Susan understood that she needed some boundaries in her life and had the courage to establish them. It worked out for her enough that she was invited to participate in a development program that only 2 percent of the people in her company at her level got to attend.

There are two steps you need to take to have boundaries. The first is to recognize what they need to be for you to consistently show up at your best at home, at work, and in the community. The second step is once you have boundaries, let other people know what they are. Let's go a little deeper on each step.

Step 1: Know Your Boundaries   Caroline Starner, Oakley's senior vice president of global human resources, is one of my role models for how to take care of yourself (remember that the only person who's really going to do that is you). By just about any measure she's had a very successful career, and I would suggest that one reason she has been successful is that she's so clear about what her boundaries are. I'll let her speak for herself on that:

> I have a pretty strong separation between work and life. I enjoy what I do, but work is a means to an end. It is not my most favorite hobby as it is for some people, and so I really am conscious about how much time do I devote to work, how much do I let work drive my life, and I am pretty segmented.
>
> So, when I'm off, I'm off. When I'm on, I'm on. So I am not doing personal things when I'm here, but I'm not doing work things when I'm home and when I'm with family and friends. It's a little bit harder in bigger positions because you are pretty perpetual, so even then I have a clear boundary of how I am going to manage e-mails when I'm on vacation, whether or not I'm going to allow myself to take conference calls, whether I'm going to take

work with me on a vacation to get something done, whether I'm taking work home at the end of the night.

If the idea of boundaries doesn't resonate with you, try thinking about what the guardrails need to be in your life. Just like the ones on a highway, the guardrails in your life are the things that keep you from running off the road. That's how Hilton's Chris Nassetta thinks about it. His job requires travel three or four days a week, and it's often international. With six kids in his family and four still living at home, one of Nassetta's guardrails is, with rare exception, to be home every Friday night. From there, Nassetta says,

> I try to dedicate my weekends to my family: going to soccer games, going to movies, cooking for my family and friends, trying to make sure that we have real time as a family together. [When I'm in town on weeknights], I like to have dinner a couple of nights a week with my kids. I could fill every single night I'm in town with business dinners and other commitments, but I consciously don't do that. As you can imagine, there is no end to the requests that come in, so I tell my assistant the same rule: life gets going so fast, if you don't have a couple of these guardrails that you use, it will get away from you and . . . without that balance between your personal and professional life, you just don't perform as well.

Step 2: Let People Know Your Boundaries   For boundaries and guard-rails to make any difference for you, you have to take step two, which is to let people know what they are. As Caroline Starner told me, making your boundaries clear can take some courage and finesse. If your boss or a colleague calls you at home at 9:00 PM, politely ask if it's urgent or if it's something that can wait until first thing the next day. If the non-urgent calls continue, let them go to voice mail and respond the next day. Starner suggests that if you respond with, "'Hey, boss, I got your call last night. I was with my family having dinner,' and you make it the first priority next day, you'll start to train them into knowing what your routines are." The same principle applies to e-mails, by the way.

As the guy in the opening story of this book said, "The first time you answer an e-mail at 2:30 in the morning, they know they've got you."

Time Tip 8: Use Yes and No Strategically

One of the quickest ways to end up feeling overworked and overwhelmed (and burned out, resentful, and depleted) is to mindlessly say yes to every request. By mindlessly, I mean not stopping to consider, investigate, or negotiate your options. I also mean not stopping to consider how the request for your time, attention, efforts, and energy ties back to the outcomes that are most important to you at home, at work, and in the community. Granted, sometimes those outcomes will be in conflict with each other in terms of how you allocate your time and attention, but it's a good idea to at least consider the request in that context. Based on how you strategically sort things through, the range of answers could be:

- A flat-out "yes"
- A flat-out "no"
- A qualified "yes, if"
- A "yes, but not right now"
- A "no, but what if . . . ?"

Don't be afraid to negotiate an approach that will meet the needs of the requestor while still honoring your needs. All too often, we ignore the opportunity to learn more about what's underneath the request and what the other person is really looking for. For instance, Caroline Starner once had an employee who told her one morning that she had missed a planned dinner with her grandmother the night before because she stayed late to work on a budget project that Starner asked her to do. Starner's response was,

> You need to tell me that and negotiate. You can say to me, "Hey, how soon do you need that? I had dinner plans with my grand-mother tonight. Should I cancel those to get this done, or can I deliver this to you in the morning?" You need to tell me those things because my expectation is never that you are sacrificing on the family side or the personal side of things to get something done, particularly if there is a quick turnaround. You have to draw the box and you have to say, "These are the things that I will not sacrifice for work."
>
> It's okay to say, "No, I can't do that. I need to take care of myself."

Sometimes the answer is just plain no because you're in it for the long run and not the short run. For instance, Crystal Cooper of Unisys could probably go to a colleague or client dinner almost every evening. She has learned that it's okay to say, "'No, I can't do that. I need to take care of myself." It can be helpful to set situational ground rules for yourself on when you say yes and when you say no. To take another example, Anne Bryant had ground rules for herself about what evening events she attended when she was based in Washington, D.C., as president of the National Association of School Boards. Her ground rule was:

> Unless I was seated at the head table I wasn't going to any more dinners. The head table gives the organization visibility, but other than that you get stuck with one person on either side of you and you can't make much headway. So I'd always go to the receptions, cruise the place, see the members of Congress I needed to see, and come home.

Are you thinking it could be hard to say no on a regular basis? You can learn to do it. Consider the case of Adam Grant, the youngest tenured professor in the history of the Wharton School and the author of the *New York Times* best-selling book *Give and Take*. When his book came out in 2013, the *New York Times Magazine* ran a long feature article that implied Grant spent most of his days "giving"—by responding to requests for advice, meetings, connections, expertise, and so on—and very little "taking"—in the form of having time for himself. When we did an interview for this book, I asked him how he keeps it all going. While he was very appreciative of the job the *Times* reporter did on the story about him, Grant said there were a couple of misconceptions in the article and that the biggest was "that I never say no. I say no probably dozens of times per day, and that has intensified in the past year since the book launch."

Another example comes from Elaine Hall. She is the mother of Neal, a young adult son with autism. She is also the founder of the Miracle Project, an organization that supports children with autism and their families with a holistic approach to life that includes a big dose of getting the kids involved in the arts. Hall's work led to the Emmy Award–winning HBO film *Autism: The Musical.* Since the success of the film, there are many more requests for and demands on her time. As she told me, it became overwhelming, but then she had a realization that could be helpful for anyone trying to determine when to strategically say yes or no:

> I put my faith before in other people and the company and prestige, and if my faith is what really matters, Neal and I are going to be okay. It's a constant challenge to not be overworked and not be overwhelmed and to learn to say no. There are so many people who want me to, "Come to this event, come to that event," and I have to say no. My big one for this year is I have to be able to say, "Does this support my goals and my dreams?" because I love helping people support their goals [but also need to know] how is this going to support my family, my goals, my dreams?

Time Tip 9: Tame the Distraction Dragon

Remember that statistic from the University of California at Irvine study about regular e-mail users that I cited in Chapter 1? They are interrupted *37 times an hour.* There are all kinds of ways to become overworked and overwhelmed. The distraction dragon of e-mail and other electronic forms of communication is at the top of the list for most executives, managers, and professionals who are feeling that way.

Here's a simple tip for taming that particular distraction dragon. Schedule checking your e-mail at specific times during the day and ignore e-mails for the rest of the time. For example, Per Wingerup of CBS spends only specific hours on e-mail each day. The first hour comes early in his workday, and the second hour is in the late afternoon. The hours in between are for creative and collaborative work that goes best when not interrupted by other people's priorities. When he was an agent and manager at the Bureau of Alcohol, Tobacco and Firearms, Henry Lescault built on Wingerup's approach and took it a step further. Each afternoon, he would turn on an autoreply message that said, "If this is an emergency, please call me on my cell phone because I will not be checking e-mails between 1:00 PM and 4:00 PM."

The big idea that got Lescault started on this approach was one that he learned in a Franklin Covey course on time management. As he told me:

> It's about what they call "managing the gravel" in your life, and the gravel is the e-mails, the pop-ins, the text messages, the meetings, all these things that might give the appearance of being important. They may be urgent but not necessarily important, and how do you deal with those things?
>
> If I can plan my week and know ahead of time, let's say on Sunday, what the most important things for me in that week are and stay focused on getting those things done, it really helps reduce that stress. It's about being mindful of that week, knowing each day what my most important things are and staying focused on those important things because the gravel doesn't go away. . . . It's not about eliminating it; it is about managing it.

One of the most important things you do to keep yourself out of chronic fight or flight mode is to stay out of the cycle of reacting all day to all the items that appear in your in-box. Most of them don't matter, but all of them can distract you if you let them. Tame those dragons by walling them off and dealing with them on your schedule not theirs.

Time Tip 10: Consider Your Impact

Several years ago I worked with a manager named Mary who was a participant in one of my company's group coaching programs. Mary was pretty amazing, actually. She was going through chemotherapy at the time of the program and had lost all of her hair. Even with all that was going on in her life and body, her energy and enthusiasm were through the roof. She was inspiring.

She was also driving her team crazy. When we ran the 360-degree assessment for the group, Mary's scores on behaviors related to micromanagement and pacing herself were really low. Her lowest item, like so many professionals I've worked with, was about pacing herself by building in breaks from work. She had one of the lowest scores I've ever seen on that behavior. When we got on the phone to review her feedback and choose a couple of behaviors to focus on for her development plan, I felt sure that pacing herself would come up. Mary didn't even mention it. There were a lot of other things she was interested in working on, but pacing herself was not on her radar screen.

So I gently brought it up. "Mary," I said, "your score on pacing yourself by building in breaks from work is pretty low. What do you think about that?"

She practically snorted out a laugh and said, "Oh, I don't need to work on that. I love working all the time. My husband and I don't have any kids. He's busy with his stuff, and I love to work from home in the evenings and on the weekends, firing off the e-mails. I get energized by it."

"Mary," I replied, "I get it that you don't need or want any breaks. Understood. Have you ever thought, though, that maybe your team needs a break from you?" She paused, said she'd never thought about it that way and could see my point. That was the beginning of a shift for her. (By the way, I saw Mary recently. She beat the cancer, has a full head of hair, is rocking and rolling and even giving herself and her team regular breaks.)

Mary was what Caroline Starner refers to as a work hobbyist. "Work is their hobby, and they love it more than anything."

Maybe that's you. If you've made a conscious choice to be a work hobbyist and that's working for you, bravo. If you've unwittingly ended up in that place, then you may want to consider the mindfulness alternative. Either way, if you're in a position of leadership in your organization, consider your impact. If you're in a leadership role, people are taking their cues from you whether you know it or not. If you're sending out e-mails late at night just because that's your thing or it's the most convenient time to do it, consider stopping that. There are people in your organization who are going to be jumping for their smartphones at 11:00 PM because the boss just sent an e-mail even though you would have been perfectly happy to get a response the next day. Likewise, if you're calling a morning meeting, consider that people may have kids to get to school, may want to get a workout in, or could just use another 30 minutes of sleep. Former GE Appliances CEO Jim Campbell told me that he regularly asked his staff to push meeting start times back from 7:00 AM to 8:00 AM so people "could get some time in the morning to go to the gym or whatever they wanted to do." The same principle applies to when you leave the office. If you stay late, they're going to stay late. You can continue to work from home if you want to, but as Admiral Thad Allen noted in my conversation with him, "They won't leave until 30 minutes after you leave. I tried to religiously leave no later than 5:00 PM. If I had work to do, I had a computer in my house. You've got phones and everything else, so there are very few things that you can do at work that you couldn't do at home."

It's true that when it comes to managing your life and work in a more mindful way, ultimately, the only person who's going to take care of you is you. If you're the designated leader in your organization, though, you can either make it harder or easier for people to do that. It's in your interest and theirs if they do.

So we've just reviewed 10 possible ways that you can make and honor a commitment to creating space for the mindfulness alternative by managing your time. If you stop to think about it, you can certainly come up with other tactics and strategies that would work well for you. Good, do that. Just don't take on more than one or two new strategies at once. As we'll discuss in the opening chapter of Part Three, it takes some time to groove and master new routines. You don't want to overwhelm yourself further with the complication and self-induced pressure of mastering a bunch of new time management routines. Pick one or two, master those, declare victory, and move on to another tactic or strategy that will work for you. Please do pick one or two to get started with, though, because when it comes to creating the space you need in your life to pursue the mindfulness alternative, the only person who's going to take care of you is you.

Coach's Corner

- What will it take for you to make a commitment to manage your time so you show up at your best?

- Whose help and support do you need? What request do you need to make of them?

- Which of the 10 time management tips is most in the sweet spot between easy for you to implement and likely to make a difference?

- What other time management hacks do you need to implement?

Part Three

7 You Are What You Repeatedly Do

How the Right Routines (for You) Help You Show Up at Your Best

Happy Hour Starts at 6:00 AM

For Alanson Van Fleet, a senior executive in a global financial services company, happy hour starts at 6:00 AM. No, he doesn't start his day with a Bloody Mary or a mimosa. Happy hour is Van Fleet's term for the morning routine that helps him show up at his best for the rest of the day. Here's his breakdown on what's in his happy hour and what it does for him:

What You'll Learn in This Chapter

- How the right routines for you support your mindfulness alternative
- Seven principles for choosing the routines that work for you
- How to get started with routines that stick

I spend the first 60 minutes of the day really focusing on taking care of myself. First, it's 20 minutes of pretty vigorous exercise. I've got an exercise bike, and I go almost at a sprint level on the bike for 20 minutes. It wakes my body up and gets my circulation going. Then I set a timer for 20 minutes of reading material related to a mindful way of life. Then I wrap up with 20 minutes of meditation.

Then I head down for breakfast and a shower and get ready for work. Happy hour sets my day up with an incredibly positive frame of mind that leaves me feeling very connected with my mind, body, and spirit. It's just a great way to start the day. . . . It carries me through.

As we begin Part Three, we turn to identifying the routines that will help you strengthen your mindfulness alternative by reinforcing how you are at your best. Just like how you are at your best is unique to you, the routines that will help you show up at your mindful best will be unique to you as well. Your routines may not look anything like Van Fleet's happy hour. They may not even take up an hour of your day, but there are undoubtedly some that would make a big difference to your best case performance and the kinds of outcomes you hope for at home, at work, and in the community. This opening chapter of Part Three is intended to give you a framework and a starting point for selecting the mindful routines that will work best for you. Once we've set that foundation, in the next four chapters we'll get into more details and ideas about the physical, mental, relational, and spiritual routines you want in your life.

If you're creating your own Life GPS as you read this book, you'll want to have your worksheet nearby as you read through Part Three. You can download a copy of the Life GPS worksheet at ootma.eblingroup.com.

Why Do Routines Matter?

Just about everyone has routines in their lives. You probably wake up at more or less the same time each weekday. You may have a routine of skipping breakfast, or perhaps you eat the same thing every day. If you go to an office every day, it's likely that you take the same route daily. Your calendar probably has some routines embedded in it, like standing meetings or conference calls. You get the idea. Human beings make an almost countless number of decisions every day. The range I've read online starts at 612 on the low end and tops out at 35,000 on the high end. Whatever the actual number is, when you stop and really break down everything you do in a given day, you realize there are a lot of decisions. It's a good thing that we have a lot of routines because if you actually had to stop and consciously think about every decision you make in a day, it would lead to a literal case of paralysis by analysis.

So routines are a good thing until they are no longer a good thing. You reach that tipping point when the routines you have no longer serve you. When was the last time you stepped back and took a look at the routines you go through most days to ask if each of them is really in service of your showing up at your best? Chances are, it's been awhile.

That's what we'll be working on over the next several chapters by asking:

> *What are the routines that I either have in my life already or need to add to my life to enable me to show up at my best more often than not?*

By focusing on the routines that add value, it will be easier for you to identify and change the routines that reduce value. The good routines will begin to crowd out the bad ones.

It comes back to that favorite Aristotle quote I cited in Chapter 4, "We are what we repeatedly do. Excellence, then, is not an act but a habit." For our purposes, excellence represents you at your best. Habits are the consciously chosen actions that make up the routines that help you show up at your best.

An example of how this works comes from Crystal Cooper, the Unisys vice president we met in Chapter 6. The day I interviewed her, she mentioned that she was two or three business days away from an important presentation that she and her team had not yet nailed down. When I remarked that she seemed really calm and peaceful about that, she told me that she had learned enough about herself over the years to know that she would get everything done in time and that it was all good. (She was right. When I e-mailed her a few weeks later to ask how things went with the presentation, she reported, "We did a great job, and it was a good day.")

In our interview, Cooper told me that the routines she's followed over the years enable her to be calm in a deep way, "How you feel internally is how you will present externally," she told me. She continued, "It's very hard to be calm on the outside if you're not calm on the inside. For me, that comes from daily routines. . . . Through them, I realized that it's all in me. I have it. The routines get me to a place where I can access that creativity and be calm and confident so that I can do these things."

Daily yoga and meditation are at the heart of the routines that enable Cooper to show up in the calm, confident, and creative state that represents her at her best. She told me, "I started off on a fairly irregular basis, and then it got to a place where I needed to incorporate it every day in the morning or, based on whatever my day was going to be like, I was able to pick 20 minutes, or half an hour, or 15 minutes, just depending on how I was feeling that day." She has found that by coming back to these routines for some period of time each day, she is not only able to set her energy level and pace but also able to clarify what she wants to accomplish in a given day.

Again, as your routines may be different from Alanson Van Fleet's daily happy hour; they may be different from Crystal Cooper's daily base touch with yoga and meditation. The point isn't to advocate specific routines but to help you identify a few that will enhance the level of mindfulness you need to bring a focused sense of awareness and intention to your life.

There's a lot of ancient wisdom that speaks to the law of cause and effect. From the Bible, we get the maxim "you reap what you sow." In Eastern religions, such as Hindu and Buddhism, the law of cause and effect known as karma plays a central role. A more contemporary and secular way to express the same idea is the principle from computer programming known as garbage in, garbage out. All these ideas have the same basic principle at their core: Actions have consequences. By establishing routines of actions that support your best case performance, it's more likely that you'll be happy with the consequences that are created in your life at home, at work, and in the community.

Seven Principles for Choosing and Following the Routines That Work for You

In almost 15 years of leadership coaching and education, I've learned a lot about what works and what doesn't work when it comes to making meaningful personal change. As you consider, choose, and follow the routines that will work best for you, here are seven principles that have proved useful to my clients and students.

1. *Strive for rhythm, not balance.* One of the most popular and commented upon posts that I've ever written for my blog was titled, "Why I Don't Believe in Work-Life Balance." As I wrote then, if you're an executive, manager, or professional with a demanding job, you're about as likely to find balance as you are to be a purple unicorn. The reason is that the world and life are both fast moving and ever changing. In that environment, balance, at best, is a temporary and fleeting state. Instead of seeking balance, try finding a rhythm instead. By focusing on rhythm, you acknowledge there are times when your pace is going to be much more oriented to work, home, or community and there are times when the counterpoints of the other aspects of your life come to

the fore. Shifting from the mind-set of balance to the mind-set of rhythm allows you to take the pressure off yourself. You have permission to quit seeking that holy grail of perfect balance. That applies to your routines as well. Some days you'll be able to spend an hour or more on those healthy routines; some days, 15 minutes or less. There may even be days when you miss them completely. On those days, take heart. One day does not a rhythm make.

2. *Start where you are.* Your routines have to work for only one person—you. As you choose your routines, be okay with starting where you are. (Where else would you start, after all?) Don't compare yourself to where others are on their journey. The important thing is to start.

3. *Feed your sweet spot.* Look for routines that help you keep the strengths that represent you at your best in the sweet spot. The goal is not to underserve or overserve your strengths but to keep them in an optimal state. For example, if, when at your best, you are really energetic, you may want to incorporate some routines that also help calm you down a little bit. After all, energetic when dialed too far to the right can look like mania. Ideally, your routines will help you dial in your at your best strengths at the sweet spot.

4. *Choose what is easy to do and likely to make a difference.* As you choose your routines, think of an *x-y* graph where the vertical axis is labeled "easy to do" and the horizontal axis is labeled "likely to make a difference." You want to choose routines that are in the upper right-hand corner of that graph—relatively easy to do and likely to make a difference. There are plenty of really hard to do routines that you could choose that might make a difference. The problem is they probably won't because it will be too hard for you to stick with them. Start with the easy ones. You'll master those soon enough, and the ones that were more challenging will seem easier at that point.

5. *Ditch the dogma.* There are best practices and then there's dogma. Pay attention to the best practices, and ditch the dogma. You'll know the best practices because they're backed up by research and proven results. You'll recognize the dogma when you pick up on a rigid or condescending attitude about how you're doing things. Dogmatism is an energy drainer. Ditch it.

6. *Take baby steps.* Through the experience of coaching others and observing myself, I've learned that baby steps are cool. You don't have to take my word for it, though. The Japanese manufacturing process that changed global manufacturing is called *kaizen* and is based on the same idea—continuous improvement through small steps. Sometimes the progress that comes from those small baby steps is so slow and incremental that it's indiscernible. And then, suddenly and without warning, one day you're doing it. It's all those baby steps that get you there. Keep taking them.

7. *Remember that less is more.* There might be 10 new routines you want to incorporate into your life. Ignore eight or nine of them— at least for now. It's far better to go deep on one or two new routines that groove themselves into your life than it is to go broad and have them skip through your life like a flat stone on a pond. By choosing only one or two new routines to start with, you raise your chance of success and the motivation to keep going. You'll also be surprised at how much of an impact those few routines have on many different aspects of your life. As long as those few new routines are relatively easy to do and likely to make a difference, it almost doesn't matter which ones you start with. They're all good.

How to Get Started on Routines That Stick

The principle of creating positive change through routines goes back to at least the ancient Greeks. They had a word *praxis,* which, roughly translated, means the act of becoming a certain way by regularly doing the discrete things that someone who is known for that quality regularly does. For instance, if, in the relational domain, your goal was to be more loving and compassionate toward your partner and children, a good place to start would be to identify some simple behaviors that are relatively easy to do and likely to make a difference.

Of course, you'd want to be consistent with that simple, easy to do behavior so that it actually makes a difference in terms of how close and connected you are with the rest of your family. To be consistent, you need a trigger or a cue—a reminder basically—to practice that behavior on a routine basis. It's a process that Charles Duhigg brilliantly described in his best-selling book, *The Power of Habit*.[1] It's a cycle of cue, routine, and reward. The cue reminds you to practice the behavior. When you do, if that action leads to a routine or consequence that feeds or serves you in some way, you have an incentive to do it again. The cycle continues to repeat itself, and pretty soon you have a new habit.

Patricia's Story

Here's a real-life example of how it works. In talking about routines at a presentation earlier this year, I asked the audience if they had any routines in their life that they had been intentional about starting and how it was working for them. A woman named Patricia offered to share her story. The last step of her commute home from work every evening is pulling her car into the garage of her house. As she walks from the garage through the laundry room and into the kitchen, she takes her smartphone out of her purse and plugs it into a charging cord that hangs over the washing machine. She leaves her phone on the lid of the washing machine, closes the laundry room door, and doesn't head back for her phone until her kids have gone to bed. That routine gives her two or three hours a night to be fully present with her husband and children. She related that it was a little challenging to get used to not having her phone on her person for the first few weeks but that the payoff was so great that parking the phone in the laundry room quickly became a habit.

You see how she is using the cue/routine/reward cycle, right? The cue for Patricia is walking into her laundry room and seeing the phone cord hanging over the washing machine. The routine is plugging her smartphone in and leaving it there until her kids go to bed. The reward is the connection that comes from sharing her undivided presence and attention with her family each evening. It's a self-reinforcing loop of a routine that's relatively easy to do and has definitely made a difference for Patricia.

There's a powerful element at play in Patricia's experience that we haven't talked about yet. That's the power of getting other people involved in supporting and reinforcing the routines you're trying to groove. There are two steps in that process. First, tell them what you intend to do so they can help hold you accountable to yourself through gentle (or maybe not so gentle) reminders. Second, ask them to help you groove the behavior. That help could be serving as behavioral cues for you, sharing ideas that will help you fine-tune those easy to do, make a difference behaviors, or letting you know what difference your new routine is making for them.

Doug's Story

For a work-based example of how getting other people involved can help you build and groove routines that will help you show up at your best, consider the story of Doug. When I was coaching Doug, he was leading a team working on a $20 million project that was deep red on a green, yellow, red status reporting system. When I conducted an opening 360-degree assessment for him, one of his lowest-rated behaviors from his direct reports was "Demonstrates an understanding of his comments and actions on the morale of the organization and makes appropriate choices." In the open-ended comments part of the report, a few direct reports mentioned that Doug was basically Debbie (or

Doug) Downer in the weekly project status meetings. It didn't matter if there were some things that were going right; all Doug focused on was the things that were going wrong. As a result, the morale of the project team was in the basement.

To his credit, Doug owned the feedback. With my encouragement, he brainstormed with his team about easy to do, likely to make a difference routines he could come up with to turn things around. The one that they agreed on was that when Doug started going totally negative in a project meeting, they were allowed to hold up three fingers as a sign that he was doing it again. (We all agreed that three fingers was better than one particular finger!) In the first couple of weeks of this practice, Doug was surprised by how often he saw the three fingered salute (which raised his level of mindfulness by making him more aware). In the next couple of weeks, Doug noticed that he wasn't getting the sign as often. He also noticed that the meetings were improving. Encouraged by that, he started thinking before the meetings about positive points he wanted to emphasize in addition to calling out the problems that needed to be solved. (The intentional aspect of mindfulness came into play.) The team started participating more. Ideas flowed. After a few months, there was no need for the signal to Doug from the team. He had formed a routine that helped him become a more mindful leader. Was the routine easy to do? Yes, definitely. Did it make a difference? Apparently so. By the end of Doug's six-month coaching engagement, the project status was green and his team gave him much higher scores on his overall and behavioral effectiveness in a follow-up survey. Moreover, he told me later that he noticed that the changes he had made in how he showed up at work were making a difference in how he showed up at home as well.

A Preview . . .

In the next four chapters, we'll focus on identifying the routines that could work for you in strengthening your mindfulness alternative.

Each chapter will focus on routines and best practices in one of four domains: physical, mental, relational, and spiritual. They're presented in that order because one sets you up for the next. Without the energy, stamina, and health that come from the physical domain, it can be challenging to show up at your best in the mental, relational, and spiritual domains. If your mental domain is full of chatter and distractions, the relational and spiritual domains will likely suffer. The strong connections you build when you're functioning at your best in the relational domain can help you make bigger picture connections about your purpose through regular spiritual routines.

As we discuss each of those domains, it will quickly become apparent that the lines between them can blur. There is definitely some overlap across the domains in terms of the routines you might decide are important for you to incorporate in your life. That's actually a good thing because it's a source of leverage in how spend your time and attention. For instance, a regular routine of a daily walk could touch all four domains. The physical benefits are obvious, and the mental benefits of giving your mind a chance to push the reset button are pretty apparent to most people as well. If you make walking with a friend, colleague, or family member part of your routine, it has relational benefits as well. Finally, for lots of people, a walk in a beautiful or inspiring natural setting can be an important spiritual routine. So there you go—one simple routine can touch four different domains of human experience. With a little bit of thinking time, you can undoubtedly come up with other routines that would reinforce how you are at you best through touching on two, three, or even all four domains. I'm here to help you figure that out. In each of the next four chapters, I'll offer a Killer App—one thing you should do in that domain if you're not going to do anything else. I'll also sprinkle in some Habit Hacks that are simple, quick, easy to do routines in each domain that could make a difference in the connection between how you are at your best and the outcomes you're hoping for at home, at work, and in the community.

. . . and a Promise

Consider a promise of spending a total of a few hours a week on routines that would strengthen the connections that move you from overworked and overwhelmed to the mindfulness alternative. The likelihood is that you'd live longer, think more clearly, and be happier and more fulfilled. Oh, yeah, and you'll get more stuff done.

Are you feeling excited or daunted about the prospect of getting started? It's natural to feel a bit of both. Don't be nervous. Just keep in mind the advice of my personal physician, Dr. Myles Spar. With a medical degree from the University of Michigan as well as training in Chinese medicine, Dr. Spar is an expert in the practice of integrative medicine. He's literally written the book on integrative health for men. When I asked him for his one best piece of advice for the overworked and overwhelmed person who wants to get off the gerbil wheel, he offered this deeply technical advice: "Fake it until you make it." Sounds like a modern day version of what Aristotle said: "We are what we repeatedly do. Excellence, then, is not an act but a habit."

Let's go build some habits and routines that will create your mindfulness alternative.

Coach's Corner

- Which of the seven principles for choosing and following the routines that work for you resonates the most? Why does it?

- Which of the seven principles will be most challenging for you to follow? Why will it?

- Who are the people in your life who have regular lines of sight into how you show up and who you'd like to invite to help you follow through on your routines?

8 It Starts with the Body

The Physical Routines That Make You More Mindful

A Crisis and a Wake-Up Call

Jane (named change to protect her privacy) started with her financial services company right out of law school and quickly moved through the ranks. With her education as an attorney and a role in international human resources, she took pride in being the go-to person when a colleague needed an answer to a tough question or a solution to a complex problem. She regularly worked 12-hour days along with time

---

What You'll Learn in This Chapter

- Why physical routines are the foundation for your mindfulness alternative

- The Killer App of physical routines that you can do almost anywhere at any time

- How two other physical routines can strengthen your mindfulness alternative foundation

---

on the weekends. It was typical for her to travel internationally three weeks a month. She was a specialist in the human resources aspects of mergers and acquisitions, and her company was doing more and more of those. Every time a new deal was announced, Jane was on the integration team, and she found the work "all consuming." She loved what she was doing, though, and took on a succession of bigger jobs with more and more scope.

Then came the biggest deal of all, and Jane was on the team that saw it through to a successful conclusion. Then she crashed.

A chronic autoimmune disease that had afflicted generations of Jane's family members suddenly showed up in her life. "The one thing you're not supposed to do when there's a propensity for this disease in your family is work yourself to death," she told me. That's what Jane almost did, though. In her words, "The lack of sleep, not eating correctly, not having time to exercise, working a god-awful lot of hours, plus just the stress of the work" forced Jane off the field. "I had always thought I dealt with stress fairly well," she told me, "but that was an extremely stressful time and situation."

That health crisis was the moment of truth that led Jane to her mindfulness alternative. The good news is that today, thanks to incorporating into her life the healthy routines that she had ignored previously, Jane's autoimmune condition is under control and she hasn't had a relapse in years. She's also still with her company and is in an even bigger role. Another difference in her life is that she's made a shift from being the go-to person to building and leading a team of go-to people. When I asked her how her colleagues would compare post-illness Jane with the pre-illness version, she laughed and said, "They would probably say, 'She is a lot more relaxed. She is not as likely to start with no and is more likely to listen.' They would probably also say, 'Her sense of humor comes out a lot more now.'"

Living and working in a state of chronic fight or flight led to a life-changing health crisis for Jane. Fortunately, she learned how to counterbalance fight or flight by nurturing her rest and digest response. Today, by pursuing her mindfulness alternative, she's showing up at her best—relaxed, open, and humorous—and has quite a fulfilling life not just at work but at home and in her community as well. All of that started when she mindfully changed her routines.

The goal of this chapter and the next three is to introduce you to the routines that might help you avoid a health crisis of your own and that strengthen the possibility of you showing up at your best. Since your physical health is the foundation for everything else you do in life, we'll start by unpacking the physical routines that could be relatively easy for you to do and that would definitely make a difference in your life. You may be doing all of these already. If that's the case, bravo; keep it up. There may be some ideas in this chapter that spark some ideas for fine tuning on your part. On the other hand, you may not be doing any of these. If that's the case, how exciting it is that you've got the opportunity to start making a few changes in your life that will probably extend it. In this chapter, as in the next three, we'll explore some basic routines that you might consider incorporating into your Life GPS. They're all designed to help you strengthen your own mindfulness alternative by counterbalancing the fight or flight in your life with some rest and digest activation. Let's begin with the Killer App of physical routines.

Movement: The Killer App of Physical Routines

In the last chapter, I made the case that focusing on your work-life rhythm will have a more positive payoff for you than trying to achieve work-life balance. One of the reasons why is that rhythm is a big factor in activating the rest and digest response that can keep you in the zone of the mindfulness alternative. In years of study and research on "the relaxation (rest and digest) response," Harvard's Dr. Herbert Benson has learned that the rhythmic repetition of a "sound, word, phrase, prayer or movement" is the first and critical step in activating the parasympathetic nervous system.[1] The last word on that list of triggers, *movement,* is the Killer App in the physical domain of routines.

There are some big reasons why movement, especially forms such as walking, running, cycling, Jazzercise, Zumba, yoga, and light weight lifting that have a repetitive rhythmic element to them, is the Killer App of physical routines:

- *Movement helps your body get rid of the stress hormones* such as cortisol and adrenaline that can be lingering around when you're in a state of chronic fight or flight.

- *Movement can be free and portable.* You can do it anywhere at almost anytime. Whatever you can do and for however long you can do it, movement will make a positive difference for you.

- *Movement can get you out of your head* by giving your mind something else to focus on other than your thoughts. As Caroline Starner said to me, movement "interrupts the chaotic mind and [can get you] singularly focused. It's really hard to work out, particularly with weights, and still be thinking about your problem."

- *Movement can make you more productive.* You may have seen or read about the growing prevalence of treadmill desks that are equipped with a special shelf for a computer keyboard and display to allow the user to walk at a two-mile-per-hour pace while working. A yearlong study of finance workers using treadmill desks found that, after an initial learning curve, their productivity on things like quantity and quality of work and quality of colleague interactions went up by a significant amount.[2] If you have or have had a routine of regular movement in your life, you likely agree with the observation of Evolent Health CEO Frank Williams who says, "Whatever time I invest in exercise, I get four times back in terms of energy and productivity and all of those types of things."

- *Movement begets movement* or at least the ability to move. Executive, managerial, and professional jobs can be physically demanding in sneaky ways. As Lynn Pendergrass, worldwide chairman for consumer products at Johnson & Johnson, told me, "When I travel for my job or even just walk through Penn Station lugging my computer up and down the steps, I wonder how people do these high-powered jobs if they're not in shape." Regular movement builds the stamina, strength, and energy you need to move through your demanding life.

- *Movement builds your confidence.* This is something I've noticed in my own practice of yoga over the past four years. I've found that the confidence I've built on the mat through newfound strength, flexibility, and balance stays with me throughout the day. Indiegogo cofounder and chief customer officer Danae Ringelmann has observed the same thing with her workouts. She shared a story with me about a tough discussion she had with a colleague that made her frustrated and angry. Instead of reacting, she went to the gym. "It was in the process of doing sit-ups," she told me, "that I remembered that I do have a core and when I mess up, I'm not going to let that one thing define my whole sense of worthiness."

That last quote from Ringelmann brings us back to the first point about movement. To even make the metaphorical connection with her core, she had to clear out the stress hormones that flowed from the fight or flight state triggered by the argument. Movement helped her do that.

What Kind of Movement Routine Is Best for You?

What kind of movement routine is best for you? That's easy—the one you're likely to do. As we've just discussed, any type of movement is

Habit Hack
Share Your Routines

Sharing your routines with a partner, friend, or colleague is a great way to kick-start your physical routines and sustain your momentum. You're much more likely to show up for a workout, a run, or a class when you know someone is there waiting for you. You don't have to limit yourself to one person. Look for groups you can join that are following the same physical routines that you are. No groups close by? Look for ones online where you can share your progress, share notes, and cheer each other on.

likely to make a difference for you. As far as your likelihood to do it, you'll want to consider factors such as how much time you have available, your current physical capabilities, cost, and what you find fun and interesting. Your routine could be something that requires some planning like going to a yoga class or the gym, or it could be something you can do on a moment's notice, such as walking around your office complex or neighborhood. (The planning and moment's notice routines are not mutually exclusive by the way. You can do both.)

You have a lot of options. If you're easily bored, you can follow the example of my physician, Myles Spar, who schedules a bike ride, a swim, strength training, or a run five days a week. (He's a triathlete. I admire him for that, but it's not for me!) Maybe a little friendly competition now and then is your thing. My friend, nutritionist Melissa McLean Jory, likes to race her mountain bike on the seniors circuit. She shared a funny story with me about how that worked out for her in her last race:

I do one race each year, and it's an all-women's race. They have 300 women, and they write your age on your calf in big black letters. And I'm in an age category where I'm literally the last person. I'm the oldest out of 300 women.

The first time I went, I was like, "Really? You have to put my age on there?" Now I'm kind of like, "Who cares?" I want to do well for myself, but I don't really care, whereas if I was 25, I would have wanted to actually win. Those kinds of things change, and it's more enjoyable. It's fun. I think that next year I might have the guy write, "32 × 2" on the back of my calf instead of 64.

For Novo Nordisk senior vice president Andy Ajello, flexibility (in more ways than one) is the key to making his routine of movement work for him. The basics for him include 30 minutes a day of cardio on a treadmill, elliptical, or bike, followed by 15 or 20 minutes of stretching, which he finds "makes a big difference." In addition to the stretching, Ajello is flexible on his timing. If he's working from his office, he usually hits the gym for 45 minutes on the way home from work. If he's on the road, as he often is in his job, he tries his best to stay in a hotel with a decent workout room: "The bottom line there is that you get up in the morning to do it because you save the time of having to drive to work," he said. "When you're there for meetings and dinners with colleagues or customers, exercise helps keep you energized and focused and not just going through the motions the next day."

Don't let the examples of triathlon training, bike races, and working out and stretching in the gym scare you off. Adding a brisk walk or two to your day is relatively easy to do and will definitely make a positive difference for your blood pressure, weight, stress level, and risk for diseases like type 2 diabetes. Monica Oswald, who we met earlier in this book, makes it a habit to take a 20 minute walk with her dog every morning and another 20 or 30 minutes around her office campus at lunch. Anne Bryant's walking routine around her neighborhood shows how easy it can be to touch bases not just in the physical domain but also the mental, relational, and even spiritual domains as well:

I love to walk outside. I see the seasons so much more. I have my cell phone on my hip so every once in a while I take pictures of what I see. I took some wonderful pictures this fall of a tree in our neighborhood that had these brilliant red leaves. The maples this year were just amazing. I don't think it was my color-blind eyes. All of my neighbors said the same thing. There was this pile of leaves by the tree, and I took several shots. That was kind of fun.

Before we leave the Killer App of movement, I have to make a brief pitch for yoga. As I mentioned in the Introduction, regular yoga practice has played a huge role for me in successfully managing multiple sclerosis. More and more research shows that yoga can have a positive impact on your health in terms of gene expression, improvement in sleeping, reduced food cravings, and in many other ways.[3] You don't have to do headstands to get the benefits; three or four 30- to 60-minute sessions a week can make a big difference. The rhythmic repetition of yoga is a fantastic way to strengthen the neural connections that lead to a strong rest and digest response that lowers stress. With yoga's booming popularity, it's easier than ever to find a good class nearby or online. You can even give it a five-minute try in your office by checking out the video mentioned in the accompanying Habit Hack and joining me in

*Habit Hack
Yoga Anywhere,
Anytime, for Anybody*

While 60- and 90-minute yoga classes are great, there's not always time for those. The good news is you can get a boost and a lot of benefit from five minutes of yogic stretching almost anywhere at any time—your office, your house, in line, and even in the cabin of an airplane. (I've stretched in all those places. You just want to be aware of who and what's around you.)

an online yoga session. (Don't worry. You can do it in your work clothes.) Does yoga sound like too big of a challenge? You might want to investigate tai chi, which is a gentle way to get the repetitive rhythmic benefits that yoga offers. Recent research shows that it also offers significant positive health benefits.[4]

If you go to the video section of ootma.eblingroup.com, I'll lead you through two easy to do, likely to make a difference brief sessions of yogic stretching (one standing and one seated) that you can do almost anytime and anywhere you need a boost. They're super simple, no experience required routines. Give them a try. I think you'll love the stretch!

Sleep Isn't Just for Wimps

Everybody sleeps, but many overworked and overwhelmed professionals don't sleep enough. Pretty much every medical expert will tell you that 95 percent of the population needs between seven and eight hours of sleep a night and the 5 percent who don't are the beneficiaries of a rare genetic mutation.[5] However, research conducted by Gallup shows that 40 percent of Americans get fewer than seven hours of sleep at night.[6] If you're trying to fill the cup of your 168 hours a week to the brim, chances are, you're part of that 40 percent. If you are, stop pouring. Your cup is running over because you're too tired to notice.

You've probably been in conversations where people are practically bragging about how little sleep they get. That's actually kind of stupid. Based on what tons of research studies tell us, they might as well be bragging about lowering their IQ and emotional intelligence. Because a lack of sleep has the biggest effect on the prefrontal cortex, the part of the brain that controls higher order decision making and emotional regulation, that's what happens.[7] They could also brag about how they're choosing to raise their risk of heart disease, obesity, strokes, and diabetes and doubling the chance that they'll die before their time.[8]

Habit Hack
Five Tips to Get Better Sleep

With a hat tip to the good folks at the Mayo Clinic, here are five easy to do, likely to make a difference tips to help you get more and better sleep:

1. *Be consistent.* Go to bed and wake up at the same time each day—weekends, too.

2. *Don't pig out.* Limit the amount of food and alcohol (water too for that matter) that you consume two to three hours before bedtime.

3. *Ritualize it.* Establish a going to bed routine that helps you relax. Stay away from video screens. The light they emit wakes you up.

4. *Keep it cool, dark, and quiet.* If you can, keep your bedroom cool, dark, and quiet. A fan, an eye mask, and earplugs can be helpful on each of those points.

5. *Work out.* Do so earlier in the day, not right before bedtime. Movement during the day helps you sleep better.[9]

You probably wouldn't choose to go out and get blotto the night before a big presentation or an important meeting. Not getting enough sleep can have the same impact as tying one on the night before. If you Google the phrase *good sleep hygiene*, you'll find all the guidelines you need to establish a better sleep routine for yourself. Keeping a regular bedtime, staying off your smartphone or tablet in the bedroom (the light from them wakes you up and they tend to make noise all night unless you remember to change the settings), and watching what you eat late in the evening are three of my favorite tips. If you're not getting seven to eight hours of sleep a night, make a mindful choice and establish a new sleep routine.

Perhaps the nighttime sleep routine is working great for you, but you're looking for another boost that will give you a performance edge. Consider taking a nap. If you work from home, a 15- to 30-minute early to mid-afternoon nap can be a great way to boost your mindful awareness, intention, and cognitive performance for the rest of the day. Research at Australia's Flinders University and other institutions proves it.[10] If you're working in an office, finding a nap space could be a little more challenging, but more and more workplaces are offering quiet rooms for nappers. One of those is HubSpot, the Boston-based Web marketing firm. Their CEO, Brian Halligan, explained to me why he set up nap rooms in the office and why he naps three to four times a week himself:

> Your prefrontal cortex actually can't hold that much information, and it gets very full very quickly. If I'm tired, it gets full. So I take a nap, and the nap reorganizes shit in my brain and gets me going so I can take in new information and process new shit.
>
> I try to take as many naps as I can. The way I think about my work life these days is about twice a month I'll have a really good idea and then during the rest of the month I have hundreds of medio-cre ideas. Those two good ideas almost always come on the way into or out of sleep. . . . When I nap it's like I finally get my mind off the thing I'm trying to solve and it opens up to solve other problems in a way that's very surprising to me.

If your workplace isn't nap-friendly, feel free to share the Halligan quote with your boss.

Focus on Your Fuel by Eating Mindfully

This section deals with the what and how of eating mindfully. The what part of the conversation begins with true confessions. If you had snuck into the Eblin family kitchen circa 2004, you would have found lots of boxed frozen entrees in the freezer and processed meats in the fridge, and maybe some fast food leftovers. If you were hankering for a snack, you would have been interested in the bags and bags of chips and other salty treats we kept in the cabinets. Have a sweet tooth? There would have been plenty of ice cream and pudding and several tubs of nonfat fake whipped cream that you could top it off with. Thirsty? You could have had a diet soda (gotta cut calories somewhere), and if we were out of stock in the kitchen, no worries because we always kept five or six cases in the garage. (We used to chain drink cans of it back in the day and were afraid of running out.) We had what experts call the Standard American Diet. (Google it.)

Around that same time, my wife, Diane, started feeling run down. She had a lot of conversations with our doctor at the time, who didn't have a lot to offer. He suggested she talk to a therapist because she was probably depressed. It didn't feel like depression to Diane, and she kept asking him for help. Most likely to get her out of his office, the doctor referred Diane to a health coach. That was the beginning of the change in our kitchen. We all started to make changes in the way we ate. If you're planning on raiding our kitchen today, you better like fish, chicken, nuts, colorful fresh vegetables and fruit, Greek yogurt, seltzer water, and fresh gluten-free bread because that's pretty much what we have to offer. Don't get me wrong; we didn't go from the 2004 to the 2014 kitchen all at once. It was a slow process of forming a lot of new eating habits. We all feel a lot better as a result.

There's been a lot of research over the past 10 years about how a diet high in saturated fats and refined sugar (our 2004 kitchen) leads to health problems such as heart disease and type 2 diabetes. That kind of diet also impairs your cognitive ability. Conversely, the vitamins, minerals, and omega-3 fatty acids that you'd find in our 2014 kitchen reduce the chance of disease and increase the neural plasticity of the brain. What you eat is the fuel for your body and mind. It just makes sense to choose wisely.

That leads us to the how of eating mindfully. Consider starting some routines that will fuel your body well:

- Avoid eating lunch at your desk or multitasking while eating. You're more likely to make bad food choices and mindlessly eat more in the process. (Besides, if you get up from your desk to eat lunch, you'll get some more walking in.)

- Learn more about healthy snacks and drinks (you can't go wrong with water), and stock a desk drawer, your office fridge if you have one, and your briefcase with a supply so you can avoid the donuts and candy that seem to always show up at meetings.

- Set some ground rules to keep you, your team, and your family healthy. For instance, Novo Nordisk's Andy Ajello has a no-bread and no-dessert rule for company dinners that he hosts. As he told me, "Since we're a diabetes company, it just makes sense." It makes sense even if you're not a diabetes company.

Three Thoughts to Keep in Mind

As we wrap up this chapter on the physical routines of mindful moving, sleeping, and eating, let me share three final thoughts to keep in mind as you consider making some changes.

Check Your Ego at the Door

Your ego and story about yourself can get the better of you if you're not paying attention. For instance, some people make their movement routine about looking good at the expense of feeling good. Power Yoga innovator Bryan Kest asked me some great questions on this point:

> Have you ever seen a machine at the gym for your spinal cord even though after the common cold there's not a greater ailment

in all of humanity than spine problems? Why are there 20 machines for places in the body like your butt cheeks and biceps that in all of human history there's never been a problem with? Why are there no machines for the greatest problem areas in the body? Is it really a health club or is it a vanity club?

The other ego risk to watch out for is when you're moving and something doesn't feel right or hurts. Don't power through it. Stop and pay attention. Your body is trying to tell you something. Don't injure yourself by mindlessly soldiering on.

Moderation in All Things

No one is suggesting that you have to be perfect with your exercise, sleep, or eating. Some days you may decide to skip your workout, stay up late with a friend, or eat the donut or piece of chocolate. Just be mindful when you make the choice. As Aristotle said, "It is better to rise from life as from a banquet—neither thirsty or drunken." Actually, I think George Harrison said it a little better: "All the world is a birthday cake, so take a piece, but not too much."

Work with Change

It's a certainty that your physical capabilities will change over the years. Don't make life harder on yourself by ceaselessly battling the changes. The following story comes from personal experience, although I could make the same point by sharing any number of stories that others have shared with me.

For the first six months after my multiple sclerosis flared in 2009, I could hardly walk, let alone run. Being the determined Type A personality that I was, I was intent on not letting that situation stand. As soon as I could, I started running again because that's what I was, a runner, and I had been since I was 13. Even though my back hurt like hell and I would hobble for two or three days afterward, I wasn't going to give it up. It meant too much to my psyche and self-identity. I grieved over it, though, and wistfully looked at other runners gliding along as I once had. Then I started going to yoga classes because I was going stir crazy not being able to run like I used to. My first class was with an instructor named Jeanne. She told me before we started that if I came to yoga three times a week, it would change my body, and if I came more than three times a week, it would change my life. She was right on both counts. The physical, mental, relational, and spiritual benefits I've gotten from yoga far exceed any I derived from years of running and anything I might have imagined. I write that not as a dis on running or as a psalm to yoga. I write it to share an example of what can happen when you work with change rather than fight it. My hope for you is that you work with it, keep reminding yourself that baby steps are cool, and, in doing so, set the foundation for your own mindfulness alternative.

Coach's Corner

- What's the one routine in the physical domain that you're not doing now that you think would make the biggest difference to your showing up at your best?
- What kind of support or information do you need to get started? Who could help you with that?
- What might get in the way of following through on that routine and how could you work around that?

9 A Beautiful Mind

The Mental Routines That Reduce Clutter and Increase Focus

Join Me, If You Will . . .

As we begin this chapter in the mental routines that could make a difference in your Life GPS and mindfulness alternative, let's try a short thought experiment together. Imagine the following excerpt is your day.

You wake up at 6:17 AM after hitting the snooze button on your alarm clock only once. After taking a quick shower, dressing, and making yourself look presentable, you're in the kitchen by 6:40 for approximately 10 minutes of quiet time before your spouse and three kids enter stage right. Check that 10 minutes of quiet time because

---

What You'll Learn in This Chapter

- How to stop your fight or flight response
- The Killer App of mental routines that will give you greater clarity and focus
- Other routines that can help you be more mentally present

---

3 minutes later, you hear an argument break out between your fifth-grade daughter and eighth-grade son over who's getting the bathroom first. You head back upstairs to referee and hear your eleventh-grade son's alarm clock blaring. You jump into his room to shake him awake and then return to the bathroom to negotiate a schedule.

Back downstairs, you grab a cup of coffee for now and pour more into a thermal mug for your commute. There's not really time to eat at this point, so you toss a muffin into your briefcase to scarf down during the ride to work. Your spouse rushes through the kitchen on the way to the garage, and the two of you pause for three minutes of negotiation on who's chauffeuring which kid to which event for the after school activities, followed by a quick kiss good-bye. The kids hit the kitchen in a flurry. Your daughter grabs her lunch and heads out the door for her bus. Your middle schooler forgets his lunch and is still dressing himself as he runs out the door for his bus, ranting loudly about how stupid his sister is. Now that it's quiet downstairs, you can hear the alarm clock still going off upstairs and you yell at the top of your lungs for your oldest son to get his butt out of bed. You hope he makes it to school today because that last shout is all you have time for. With the traffic, if you don't leave for work right now, you're going to be half an hour late for your 8:30 AM meeting.

Backing out of the driveway, you almost run over your son's scooter and your daughter's bike. "What do we have to do to get these kids to take care of their stuff?" you mutter to yourself. As you leave your neighborhood, you realize you forgot your coffee for the road. No time to go back for it, though. At the last stoplight before the interstate, you check your phone for urgent e-mails (you know you shouldn't, but you do anyway). There's one from your boss who needs to talk with you as soon as you hit the office because a project you're working on with the London office blew up overnight. After you pull onto the interstate, you call her assistant (hands free, sort of) to see if you can negotiate a time to meet with her since you're barely going to make the 8:30 meeting on time anyway and it's also important. The assistant isn't in yet, so you leave her a message and hope she'll call you back before you get to the office. In the first thing that's gone right this morning, you find yourself with a few miles of open road ahead, so you decide to do a mental run through of the presentation you have to give to the management committee at 1:30 this afternoon. You've just thought through the open when suddenly you stop for red tail lights as far as the eye can see. Oh crap, not another "Lord knows when it will be over" traffic delay! You turn on the radio and tune to the station that has "traffic and weather on the eights." You get tuned in just as the traffic reporter is saying, "next traffic report in 10 minutes." So you sit there in stop and go traffic for the next 10 minutes, fiddling with the traffic app on your phone while wondering if you should bail out at the next exit half a mile up the road and take the side streets to the office. Then you start thinking about the one on one you have later today with the team member who's on a performance improvement plan and how passive-aggressive he was the last time you tried to coach him. Speaking of passive-aggressive, what's the deal with that mom on your daughter's travel soccer team? You're so sick of the competitive parenting that goes on with your kids' sports teams and schools that you could scream. Moving on, you notice the bumper sticker on the car in front of you that says, "My gerbil rocks" and think of the silly YouTube video of spinning gerbils that somebody posted on Facebook last night. Wait, what were you thinking about? Oh yeah, the budget report that's due tomorrow that you still don't have the numbers for. No, that wasn't it, but that is an issue.

You snap out of your thoughts when the traffic report comes back on and you learn that the snarl you're stuck in started with a major accident ahead involving two cars and a truck. First responders have shut everything down except for the far left lane, where traffic is moving through "at a crawl." You've moved up to that exit you had your eye on and bail out for the side roads. After 40 more minutes of navigating stop and go traffic, red lights, and school buses, you arrive at the office parking garage at 8:40 AM. Of course, almost everyone arrives at your office by 8:00 AM, so the only garage spots open are on the roof. You park, turn to the backseat to grab your briefcase, and realize it's sitting on your kitchen counter along with the coffee you forgot to bring. As you descend the six floors of the parking garage and walk to the building, you're doing triage in your mind of everything that's in the briefcase and how you'll navigate your day without all of the stuff that's in there.

Seven minutes later you're finally walking in the front door of the building as your phone is lighting up with not one, but two text messages— one's from your boss and one's from the person chairing your 8:30 AM meeting. They both say the same thing: "Where r u?!"

Welcome to your day.

STOP (And Do This. Seriously, Do This.)

Okay, sorry to do that to you but I wanted you to get in touch with all of the things that can clutter your mind even in the space of just a couple of hours. Perhaps your own anxiety level is up a little bit just from reading through that thought experiment. Let's clear all of that out right now.

So, after the brief instructions in this paragraph, stop reading for a few minutes to do what I'm about to request. Place one hand on your chest and the other on your belly and take three deep breaths. Inhale through your nose and exhale from your mouth. You'll know you're breathing deeply if your top hand remains relatively still and your bottom hand is moving in toward your spine as your belly contracts on the inhales and away from your spine as your belly expands on the exhales.

Go ahead; take the three deep breaths. I'll be here when you get back.

Okay, you've taken your deep breaths. Now, take a few more moments to observe how you feel. Pay attention to your shoulders, neck, jaw, and forehead just above the bridge of your nose. How do they feel? Chances are, if any of these areas were tense before the breathing, they feel a little more relaxed now. What do you notice about any change in your mental state from before the deep breathing to after the deep breathing? Are you still thinking about that overworked and overwhelmed morning from hell scenario, or have you already moved on? My guess is that your mind has already moved on. Isn't it interesting how quickly that can happen? Okay, then, we're ready to proceed.

The process we just walked through is a mainstay of mindfulness-based stress reduction programs called STOP. It's an acronym for **s**top what you're doing, **t**ake some deep breaths, **o**bserve what's going on with yourself and your environment, then gather your thoughts and **p**roceed. It's a simple way to:

- Stop your fight or flight response in its tracks
- Reduce the chatter and clear out the clutter in your mind
- Increase your focus on what's actually going on and what, if anything, you need to do about it

Dealing with the Time Frames of Mind

That's what this chapter is all about—building your mindfulness alternative by reducing mental clutter and increasing your focus. That's what makes the beautiful mind that helps you show up at your best. As we get started, let's consider what clutters your mind in the first place. The obvious answer is a whole bunch of thoughts. The Laboratory of Neuroimaging at the University of Southern California estimates that the average person has 70,000 thoughts per day.[1] It's interesting to consider what time frames of mind those thoughts are in—past, present, or future. In writing this book, I haven't been able to find reliable research that breaks down what percentage of the average person's thinking resides in each of those three time frames. If you take a few moments to get "up on the balcony" and observe your own thinking, you'll likely find that, just as in the scenario that opened this chapter, you have a rich and varied mixture of thoughts that skip around between the past, present, and future time frames. Just shifting back and forth across the three can create clutter in your mind that can leave you feeling overworked and overwhelmed.

In the past tense time frame, your mind can become cluttered with rehashing things you wish you had done differently and can get stuck in a rut of remorse and regret. In the present tense time frame, the clutter usually comes from the volume of things rushing at you that can distract you from focusing on what's most important. As for the future tense time frame, the mind clutter there is often concerned with worry-filled anxious thoughts about things that haven't happened yet and may not ever happen.

We'll take a look at three routines—one for each time frame—that can help you clear the clutter and the Killer App of mental routines that have strong positive benefits across any of the time frames. Let's begin with the Killer App.`

The Killer App of Mental Routines: Breathing

About a year before I wrote this book, I spent a good part of the summer going through a 200-hour yoga teacher training program. It wasn't because I want to make a career shift to teaching yoga full time (too much competition!), but because I found myself sneaking some stretching routines into my leadership workshops and thought I should actually learn a bit more about what I was doing. It was a lot more work than I ever imagined it would be, especially with a busy travel schedule during the week, but I hung in there, got the "Gentleman's C," and passed the course. Now, I'm a Registered Yoga Teacher and, next time we see each other, I will show you the wallet card if you want proof.

About halfway through the program, I was heading out of town for a few days to lead a Becoming a Mindful Leader workshop. I certainly had more than a few ideas about how to approach the session but was also open to ideas from folks who had been working directly in the mindfulness field longer than me. My teacher training leader, Birgitte Kristen, has 25 years of teaching yoga under her belt. She fit the bill so I asked her to lunch.

After telling her about the workshop and the group of high-potential corporate managers that would be there, I asked Birgitte what she thought I should focus on with them. Without any hesitation, she immediately said, "Their breathing; ambitious people don't know how to breathe." When I asked her what she meant, she said that pretty much every corporate type person that she has taught over the past 25 years takes very shallow breaths from their chest rather than deep breaths from their belly. (That's why I wanted you to put one hand on your chest and the other on your belly when we went through the STOP exercise earlier.)

Take a Deep Breath

For most of your life, you've probably heard people say, "Take a deep breath," to someone who's really angry or upset about something. You may have even said it yourself on occasion. It's one of those things that we hear or say so much that it's practically become a cliché and lost its meaning. You know, "Take a deep breath." "Yeah, right, like that's going to do any good" might be the spoken or unspoken response. Well, actually, it would do some good, and there's plenty of anecdotal and scientific evidence that proves it. That's why breathing is the Killer App of mental routines. It reduces the clutter and helps you focus.

From an anecdotal standpoint, you probably just experienced the mindful effects of breathing if you did the exercise at the beginning of this chapter. Breathing is the tool that's always available to you when you need to gather yourself. You may be like Jeri Finard, the CEO of Godiva Chocolatier, who has the habit of starting every meeting by taking two or three deep breaths. As she told me:

> I have to reorient myself from whatever it is that I was doing and whatever I was feeling in the last minute. This next meeting is a totally different group, and so I think I need a minute to kind of put myself back in the moment of what I need to do with these people at this time.

Community Mercy Health Partners CEO Paul Hiltz has learned to use breathing as both a way to center himself and as a sign that he needs to push the reset button and do that. When I asked him how he uses breathing as a signal to recenter, he said he notices that when he's feeling overworked and overwhelmed, his breathing becomes "a little bit faster, shallower, and it's more up in my chest than it is in my

---

Habit Hack
Breathing for People Who Don't Know How to Breathe

Of course, breathing is the price of admission for staying alive. We all have to breathe, but a lot of people forget or don't know how to breathe as a way to calm themselves and clear out the clutter. If you're really spun up in chronic fight or flight mode, it can be hard to focus on your breathing for more than a couple of breaths.

If you'll check out the breathing video on ootma.eblingroup.com, I'll lead you through a couple of short breathing routines that I guarantee you can do on your own later and that will make a difference for you even if you don't know how to breathe.

belly." That's his cue to push the reset button as he says to himself:

> Okay. Slow down. Slow down. Sit here for a minute." Some-
> times I collect myself in my office and breathe from my belly
> for two or three minutes before I go out to the next thing and
> try to think through what I'm setting out to do. I'll do a mini
> break like that.

The Science of Breathing

There's some serious science that backs up the efficacy of how
Finard and Hiltz rely on their breathing to reduce the clutter and
show up at their best. For instance, a 2011 controlled study at
India's Jawaharlal Institute of Postgraduate Medical Education &
Research showed that participants who practiced around 35 minutes
of pranayama breathing three times a week for 12 weeks showed a
significant reduction in perceived stress and significant improvement
in cognitive functions such as focused attention, visuomotor speed,
and memory retention capacity.[2] (In case you're not familiar with
it, *pranayama* is a yogic term used to describe a thousands-of-years-
old process of the kind of repetitive rhythmic breathing that
activates the rest and digest response.) The researchers concluded
that the activation of participants' parasympathetic (rest and digest)
nervous system was what led to the reduction in stress and increase
in cognitive functions.

Well, you may be thinking, that's wonderful for people who
have 12 weeks to learn a 35-minute routine that has been around
for thousands of years, but that's not my life. Okay, I hear that, so
consider a 2009 Wake Forest University School of Medicine study
in which some of the participants were asked to do a simple
meditative breathing routine for 20 minutes a day for four days
while others were asked to spend the same amount of time listening
to audio recordings of *The Hobbit*. Both groups were given a battery

of assessments on overall mood and cognitive ability before and after the four-day period. While participants in both groups were in better moods four days later (there's just something about the tales of Middle Earth, I guess), only the meditative breathing group showed improvement on the cognitive measures. Their measured ability to sustain focus was 10 times greater than that of the people who listened to *The Hobbit.*

So, what was the magic routine that enabled the meditative breathing group to score 10 times higher on focus than the people who were listening to the book? It's pretty simple actually; they focused on their breath:

> Participants were instructed to relax, with their eyes closed, and to simply focus on the flow of their breath occurring at the tip of their nose. If a random thought arose, they were told to passively notice and acknowledge the thought and to simply let "it" go, by bringing the attention back to the sensations of the breath.[3]

If you've heard of mindfulness meditation and have been wondering what it's all about, there you go. In its simplest form, mindfulness meditation is what the participants in the Wake Forest study did—close your eyes and focus on your breath. When your mind wanders to thoughts other than your breath, as it inevitably will (it happens to everybody), just notice that and come back to your breath. It's not a big complicated thing, and it's not a competition to see who can go the longest without thinking about other thoughts. It's simply a process of training your mind to recognize when it's distracted and to bring itself back to a point of focus without making a big deal out of it. Think of it like doing reps at a gym. Within reason, the more you do, the stronger you get. Mindful breathing is like a workout for your brain. Can't imagine doing that for 20 minutes? No problem; start with 10 minutes. Don't have the patience to sit still for that? Great; try five minutes. Does the thought of five minutes of quietly breathing freak you out? No worries; try it for two minutes. I'll practically guarantee you that you can do it for two minutes. I'm willing to bet that you'll get so much out of just two minutes that pretty soon you'll be focusing on your breathing for four or five minutes at a time once or twice a day. Remember, baby steps are cool. Little steps repeatedly taken lead to big results.

With some practice using the Killer App routine of breathing, you'll learn how to use it to help you throughout the day like Jeri Finard and Paul Hiltz do. It can even help you make adjustments on the fly, as it did in this real-life example from Alanson Van Fleet, the financial services industry executive we met earlier. Van Fleet was delivering an important presentation to a group of his company's most senior executives. Ten minutes or so into the meeting:

Habit Hack
Don't Mind the Time

Wondering how you're going to know when 5, 10, or 20 minutes of mindful breathing is over? Good news! There's an app for that. There are lots of different apps that you can download for your smartphone that will allow you to set it and forget it for whatever amount of time you want to set aside to breathe. Most of them have features that allow you to set chimes or other sounds at the beginning and end of the time and, if you want, at intervals throughout. Many of them also have features that let you keep track of your stats and even connect with other people who have a routine of breathing or meditation. Search for meditation timers in an app store, and you'll find an array to choose from.

[I started to realize] this was not going well, and a kind of a fear came over me, saying, "I think I am about to lose this audience and a month of work that has gone into this idea." I think because of my mindfulness practice . . . I know when fear comes into my body and it starts showing up at the back of my neck and across the shoulders. That's where I can first feel the tension. So I started feeling that and then in my stomach, so I was like, "Okay, how can I just step back even with all these eyes on me? How can I step back, take a breath, compose myself, and relax so this fear doesn't take over? And then if I can achieve that calm, I can construct how to end this presentation in a very different way than I had anticipated." So that's what I did. I breathed.

It came to me that this was not the time to close the sale. Instead, it was "let's shift gears and ask a set of questions that might come up." More of "This is a situation we are facing, ladies and gentlemen," rather than "Here is what we need to do." I just stopped using the slides and said, "With all of this in mind, what are the questions that we need to ask? How are you experiencing all of this, and what are some of the things that we can do?"

While that particular meeting wasn't a huge success for Van Fleet and his team, it also wasn't a disaster, even though it seemed to be headed in that direction. Van Fleet's long-term investment in a breathing routine that raised his level of awareness and ability to reduce his mental chatter yielded a return that enabled him to show up at something that looked more like his best that day. It also set him up to take the steps needed to put the project back on track. As Birgitte Kristen might say, it's just another example of why it's important to learn how to breathe.

Routines to Navigate the Time Frames of Mind

We'll wrap up this chapter on mental routines by focusing on some simple ones that you can use to navigate the time frames of mind: past, present, and future.

Past Tense: Reduce Regret and Remorse

Is there anyone here who has never made a mistake, blown an opportunity, or said something they wish they hadn't? Raise your hand if that's you. Hmm, I don't see any hands going up. Just for the record, I'm not raising mine either. We all make mistakes in life and do things that we regret. It's part of the human experience. Unfortunately, we can make the rest of that human experience a lot more difficult if our minds are cluttered with the remorse and regret that causes us to relive again and again stuff that's already happened. It can be debilitating. If you're in that remorse and regret place, you have to move out. Here's a three-step routine that can help you do so.

Step 1: Breathe Yes, we're starting with breathing again. And, yes, there is once again scientific evidence that demonstrates why you should start here. A 2013 study conducted by researchers from INSEAD and the Wharton School found that one 15-minute session of a focused breathing meditation (much like the ones described earlier in this chapter) enabled participants to reduce their "sunk cost bias" about decisions they had already made that didn't work out and instead focus on the options that were actually available to them in the present.[4] The research shows that the more people focus on the present moment, the less attention they pay to sunk costs. So, the first step toward reducing regret and remorse is to bring yourself more into the present by spending 15 minutes to just focus on your breathing. (Don't have 15 minutes? Try five. Don't have five minutes? Try three deep breaths from your belly.)

Step 2: Learn the Lessons The U.S. Army uses a process called an After Action Review to learn from the past and do better in the future. Another term for it is a *lessons learned analysis*. Once you've cleared the mental clutter of remorse and regret associated with stuff that's already happened (see Step 1), you can learn some lessons that will set things on a more productive path. In its simplest form, your lessons learned analysis can be organized around three simple questions:

1. What was supposed to happen?
2. What actually happened?
3. What would I do differently next time?

Think through your answers. Jot them down. Get up on the balcony and look for patterns and connections, especially on the third question.

Step 3: Take Action Now   Based on your answers to the third question in Step 2, you have some options for taking action now. And by *now,* I mean *now.* Right now is the only moment that you or anyone else has. The past is nothing more than a memory. (We'll get to the future in a little bit.) Since now is the only moment you have, it makes sense to use it to take action based on whatever you've learned from the past. What are one or two things, if any, that you want to do in the near future to mitigate what went wrong or to set things up for better outcomes in the future?

Present Tense: Playing with Presence

One of the big benefits of the breath-based mindfulness meditation routines is that they strengthen your recognition of when your mind is wandering from the present moment. Unless there's a sudden noise or other event that gets your attention, the only thing that is going on in your present moment at that point is the breathing. So, if your mind wanders from that, then it's highly likely that it's wandered back to the past tense or forward to the future tense. There's nothing wrong with either of those necessarily, but they both represent a lot of the thoughts that are likely cluttering your mind. Of course, when you're going about your normal routines throughout the day, there can be plenty of things that are coming in in real time that can distract you from whatever it is you're trying to focus on. (Remember Admiral Allen's line about the tyranny of the present and those stats about interruptions every 11 minutes and screen changes every 39 seconds?) Whatever time frame of mind you choose, the amount of thoughts that can distract you from what's happening right now can be endless.

That's why it makes sense to establish a routine of playing with presence. Here's what I mean by that. There are routine tasks that you do throughout any given day, such as brushing your teeth, taking a shower, driving to work, cooking, eating, washing the dishes, and getting ready for bed. Have you noticed that you completely zone out or multitask during a lot of those routine tasks? For instance, have you ever driven home from work and as you're pulling into your driveway or garage realize that you really weren't thinking at all about driving for the past 20 or 30 minutes? (Scary, isn't it?) Ever sped through lunch so quickly that you have a hard time remembering what you ate a few hours later? (Whatever it was, it may be why you feel so sluggish right now.)

Since you're going to do all those tasks anyway over the course of the day, why not take the opportunity to turn some of them into opportunities to build your attention muscles by playing with presence? If you're not ready to sit and breathe for 15 or 20 minutes, just being present during everyday tasks can be a great place to start. That's what works for Evolent Health CEO Frank Williams:

> Whenever I would wash dishes, all I would think about is the fact that I didn't want to be washing dishes. I'd be in a different world. When I started to just focus on the activity of washing the dishes and literally cleaning the plate, it became an immensely satisfying activity. I try to do a few activities in my day, like washing dishes

or brushing my teeth, where that's all I'm thinking about during the activity. So I'm very focused on a clear-mind presence by just focusing on the activity.

Simple, right? Why not take a moment right now to identify a routine task later today where your intention is to be fully present? If you're cleaning the pots and pans tonight, pay attention to the temperature of the water, the quality of the soap bubbles, the spots you missed in the pan on the first pass (my wife's biggest pet peeve with me), and all the other aspects of the experience. If you find your mind wandering off to that meeting you had today or the presentation you're doing tomorrow, no big deal. Just notice it, and then come back to the pots and pans. Playing with presence in little ways can help you be more present when it matters most.

Future Tense: Visualize Worry Away

When you're feeling overworked and overwhelmed, it's easy to relate to what the French essayist Montaigne once wrote, "My life has been full of misfortunes, most of which never happened." As you look at your calendar and to-do list and all of the things you haven't done or prepared for yet, it's easy to start playing the game of "what if," as in "What if I'm not ready for that meeting?" or "What if I don't get this done on time?" At times like this, it's good to remember what my educator friend, Ward Mailliard, tells his high school students: "Worry is not a form of preparation."

If you find your mind cluttered with worries about the future, it's difficult to stay focused and show up at your best. The good news in this case is that you recognize that you're worrying about the future. (If you've been sticking with your Killer App routine of breathing, there's a good chance it helped you recognize the worry in the first place.) Recognizing and being aware of the thought pattern is the first step in moving toward one that's more productive.

From there, you have a lot of options, but I'll mention two routines that can make a big difference. The first is the routine of reassessing your priorities and resetting your calendar if necessary. (See Time Tips 2 and 3 in Chapter 6 if you need a refresh on that.) The second routine, which is particularly helpful when you're anxious about something you have to do in the future, is visualization. It's actually very useful even if you're not particularly anxious but just want to show up at your best and create strong outcomes. Here's how it works.

If you've ever watched the Olympics on TV, you've seen the power of visualization in action. Gold medalists like Michael Phelps on the starting block at the pool or Mikaela Shiffrin in the gates at the top of a ski course are running through one last visualization in the moments before they begin the race. After taking a few deep breaths (there it is again) to clear their mind, they're basically envisioning the answers to two big questions that have far broader applications than sporting competitions:

- What am I trying to do?
- How do I need to show up to do that?

Asking yourself those two questions about a future event and going a little deeper with some thought-provoking follow-up questions can make a huge difference in raising your confidence level and reducing any anxious thoughts that you have about an important future event. Some good follow-up questions include:

- "What do people know, think, feel, do, believe if that conversation, presentation, meeting is successful?"
- "If I reverse-engineer back from a successful outcome, what are the critical steps for getting to that result?"
- "When I'm showing up, what does it look or sound like in terms of my energy level, my body language, my tone of voice, and other factors?"

Questions like these can also help bring you back to the present moment by identifying specific steps you can take to create successful outcomes. Try it for yourself. Pick an event on your calendar within the next couple of weeks that matters and about which you'd like to feel a bit more confident. Take a few deep breaths to clear your head, and then ask yourself the questions presented here. Better yet, ask a friend or colleague to take five minutes to ask you the questions and just allow you to think through your answers out loud. I'll bet you will have a clearer, more confident picture of the future five minutes later. I've done this hundreds of times with thousands of clients and audience members, so I know it works.

And If You Don't Mind . . .

Sorry about that headline. Couldn't resist the pun as we wrap up this chapter on the mental routines that you may want to consider to help reinforce how you are at your best and overcome the feeling of being overworked and overwhelmed.

If you follow through on nothing else from this chapter, I hope that you'll start paying more attention to your breathing and that you give yourself at least five minutes a day to sit quietly, focus on your breathing, notice when your thoughts go in another direction, and then bring them back to your breath. That's called mindfulness meditation, folks. It's not that big a deal to do but can pay huge dividends in terms of reducing your mental clutter and increasing your focus. If that's not reason enough for you to make it a daily routine, consider, as we discussed in Chapter 3, that there's Nobel Prize–winning research that shows that mindful meditative breathing can strengthen the chromosomes that determine the quality and length of your life. Again, pardon the pun, but establishing a routine of regular meditative breathing seems like a no-brainer to me. I hope it does to you too.

Choosing the routines that work best for you in the physical and mental domains can set you up for the kind of relational routines in your Life GPS that can help you create the conditions for the kind of outcomes you hope for at home, at work, and in your community. Let's take a look at some options for relational routines in the next chapter.

Coach's Corner

- What's your take? Do you usually breathe from your chest or your belly?

- What kind of cues could remind you to breathe when the fight or flight response clutters your mind?

- Which time frame of mind—past, present or future—presents your biggest opportunity for more mindfulness?

10 In Right Relationship

The Relational Routines That Connect You with the Bigger Picture

Another True Confession

Before I became a leadership coach and author, I spent 15 years as a corporate guy. The last of those corporate jobs was a four-and-a-half-year stint as the head of human resources for a subsidiary of a Fortune 250 energy company. The parent company was emerging from a period of bankruptcy, and I was recruited as part of a new management team that was going to lead a turnaround. It literally took me only the first hour of my first day on the job to realize how in over my head I was. Fortunately, my CEO was a great boss, and she coached me through a learning curve that took longer than it should have.

What You'll Learn in This Chapter

- The impact of relationships on your health and your results
- The Killer App of relational routines that will help you create more than you expected
- Other relational routines that can make a difference for you and the people in your life

---

In my first year and a half in that job, I worked as hard as I could to get the results that were expected and wasn't that concerned with making friends. I was feeling the pressure and was in a hurry to learn and make changes. Then the CEO commissioned a 360-degree assessment for every member of her senior management team. When we all got our 360 reports back a month or so later, my results were pretty easy to summarize—my team hated my guts.

That was pretty devastating for me to learn. Up to that point in my career, I had had a lot of success. To get what was essentially a failing grade on my 360 freaked me out. I hid in my office as much as I could for the next couple of weeks. After an excessive period of licking my wounds, my coach told me I needed to go ask my team members what I had done to get such low ratings. The good news is that there was a lot of consensus on what I could fix. To a person, they each said the same thing, "You make us feel like we're not important." When I asked how I was doing that, I again got a consistent answer: "Whenever we're in a meeting with you, you're constantly looking at your watch. It makes us feel like you're not listening and that you feel like you've got something more important to do."

Here's the really sad part. They were totally right—I did feel like I had something more important to do. After all, I was in a hurry and responsible for delivering a lot of important results. That was my own story at least. What I was too egotistical, naïve, inexperienced (insert your favorite word here) to realize was that whatever results I hoped to get really had nothing to do with me and everything to do with the relationships I had with my team.

That 360 was a pivotal wake-up call not just in my career but in my life. I worked hard to turn it around with my team back then and have been working on it ever since.

Of course, if we were able to magically drop 2014 technology into that story about my 360 experience in 1997, the feedback would have probably been, "Whenever we're in a meeting with you, you're constantly looking at your iPhone. It makes us feel like you feel you've got something more important to do."

What Else Suffers When Relationships Suffer

Let's all fess up at this point. You've done that, right? I've done that. On the other hand, you've probably been on the receiving end of the smartphone sneak-a-peek, too. I have. Doesn't feel good, does it? Or maybe it's just become so common that we don't even notice anymore. That's the impact of being overworked and overwhelmed and why relational routines are a key component of your Life GPS and mindfulness alternative.

The moment that crystallized that for me came a few years ago when my son and I went to a movie together. Our seats toward the back of the theater gave us a fairly sweeping view of all the rows in front of us sloping down toward the screen. What we saw from that vantage point was around 80 percent of the people in the theater twiddling with their smartphones. It seems a fair bet that 8 out of 10 people didn't go to the movies by themselves that night. Most of them were there with someone else, but the device drew their attention more than the person next to them. What do you expect, though? We're living in an age when 84 percent of people surveyed report that they could not go a day without checking their smartphones and 72 percent of Americans are never more than five feet away from their device.[1]

I see the impact of this type of nondiagnosed attention deficit disorder all the time in my work as a leadership coach, and so do my clients. When we've run our own 360-degree assessments and self-assessments for them over the past several years, performance on the behavior called "Gives others his/her full presence and attention during meetings and conversations" has been declining year over year. Relationships, and all of the important things that flow from healthy and vibrant ones, are suffering as a result of the nonstop distractions epitomized by our addiction to the smartphone. But what, exactly, suffers as relationships suffer? Here are some candidates for your consideration:

- **Your results:** Over the years, I've observed that most leadership and interpersonal behaviors fall into one of two broad categories. There are the behaviors that drive results and the behaviors that build relationships. The second category is critical to the first. Getting things done depends on people working together. To get results over the long run, you have to attend to the relationships. Just from a purely transactional standpoint, that's how things work.

- **Your health:** On a more personal level, your physical health depends on the strengths of your relationships. My physician, Myles Spar, told me that "the biggest disease-causing agent is lack of connection." The research proves him right. A 2010 meta-analysis conducted by researchers at Brigham Young University (BYU) examined the findings of 148 different studies that tracked the social habits of more than 300,000 people around the world. The BYU analysis found that people with strong relationships with family, friends, or coworkers had a 50 percent better chance of being alive after 7.5 years than people who don't have strong relationships. The meta-analysis also showed that having weak relationships is more harmful than not exercising, twice as bad as being obese, and about as bad as being an alcoholic or smoking a pack of cigarettes a day.[2] If you want to live a longer, healthier life, you need to nurture strong relationships. They're yet another way to get out of chronic fight or flight syndrome by activating your rest and digest response.

- **Your humanity:** Allow me, if you will, to get a little bit deep in this paragraph. As human beings, we can look at relationships as transactional, or we can look at them as transformational. In the former, we tend to view other people through the lens of what they can do for us. In the latter, we view them as expressions, just as we ourselves are, of whatever universal force is behind the mix of oxygen, carbon, hydrogen, calcium, and the other elements that make up the human body. Whatever it is and however you think of it, we all come from the same source. In that sense, the way we treat one is the way we treat the whole. When you look at and engage with other people and the world from the perspective of the whole, you start to change it. That's where the biggest, most interesting game is being played.

The Killer App of Relational Routines: Listening

Whenever I have coaching clients whose colleague feedback suggests they have an opportunity to improve their listening skills, I strongly encourage them to take that on. The ripple effects of being a better listener are so great and cut across all aspects of life, not just life at work. That's why listening is the Killer App of relational routines. If you can better understand your typical style of listening, what drives it, and when to use it or not use it, you'll be much better equipped to show up at your best.

A number of different models are out there that outline different levels or styles of listening. To help you connect your listening style with the mindfulness alternative, I'll offer one that outlines three different styles of listening:

- **Transient listening:** This style is all about you and shows up a lot when you're operating in a state of chronic fight or flight. It's the fly-by style of listening that you use in a true emergency, when you're distracted, or when on your way to something else.

- **Transactional listening:** This style is all about getting stuff done in conjunction with other people. Doing this effectively requires a shift out of fight or flight but doesn't necessarily require a deep level of presence.

- **Transformational listening:** This is the style that helps strengthen relationships by building connection. It opens up the opportunity for more transformative outcomes at home, at work, or in the community.

Diagnosing Your Go-To Listening Style

The first step in building some habits that will take your listening to the next level is to understand your typical starting point. To help with that, I've created a simple diagnostic worksheet presented in Figure 10.1. As you look at each of the three listening styles and the characteristics associated with them, which of the three has been your go-to style for most of the past year? Is that style consistent across the three arenas of life—home, work, and community—or are you more

	Transient Listening	Transactional Listening	Transformational Listening
Focus	Me	You	Us
Goal	Wrap it up	Solve a problem	Learn more
Quality	Distracted and Impatient	Purposeful and Focused	Creative and Connected
Tools	• Yes or no questions • Interruptions • Telling	• Open-ended questions • Next step questions • Setting timelines	• Building on what's said or meant • Listening with more senses engaged • Using the silence
Observing	What's in your head	What's said	What's not said
Outcome	$1 + 1 = 1$	$1 + 1 = 2$	$1 + 1 = 3$

Figure 10.1 Three Styles of Listening

likely to shift styles depending on the setting? Take a look at the diagnostic for a few minutes, and then we'll talk about ways to address any opportunities you identify.

So, which of the three listening styles best describes you over the past year? If you've been feeling overworked and overwhelmed, my guess is it's been primarily a mix of transient listening and transactional listening.

Profile of a Transient Listener

In the moments when you've been more of a transient listener, you've probably shown up as distracted and impatient. That's what I was back when I was constantly looking at my watch in meetings with my team. My mind was almost always on five things other than the conversation I was in. I just wanted to wrap it up and get it over with so I could move on to the next thing. To be totally honest, I was mainly a transient listener with my family back then, too, because I spent so much time being that way at work that it was hard to shift out of that when I was home. As for friends, I didn't have a whole lot of them back then because I didn't have friendship high on my list of priorities. Needless to say, the transient style isn't the greatest way to win friends and influence people. In cases like a true emergency, it has its uses, but true emergencies are usually few and far between. If transient listening is your primary style, you're going to damage your relationships to the point where you really don't have any that are true.

The first thing you need to do to make the shift from transient listening is—wait for it!—take some deep breaths. (You knew that's where I was going, right?) The reason you're a transient listener is because you're in chronic fight or flight. Now that you know what transient listening looks like, you can make a conscious choice to shift away from it. That starts with the deep breaths that will activate your rest and digest response. That will give you the space you need to visualize how you really want to show up in the next conversation. Transactional listening is a good next step goal for that.

Habit Hack
Watch Your Ratios

You may have heard that we have two ears and one mouth for a reason. Striving for a 2:1 ratio of listening to talking is not a bad goal. If you're a note taker during meetings or conversations, try keeping track of how much you listen versus how much you talk. Mark off a section of the paper and write down the names of all the people on the conference call. Whenever a person talks for more than a sentence or two, put a check mark by his or her name. That includes you, too. The visual representation of comparing listening to talking might hold some lessons for you.

Profile of a Transactional Listener

If you're viewed as someone who gets stuff done, you're probably a good transactional listener. Transactional listening is focused on the end goal of solving a problem or identifying a next step. As a skilled transactional listener, you're the master of open-ended questions such as:

1. What are you trying to do or accomplish?

2. What's going on now that supports that or is a barrier to getting that done?

3. What have you tried so far?

4. What else could you try?

5. What are the next one or two things you need to do to move forward?

6. What kind of help or resources do you need?

7. What do you need from me?

You can see from the questions that a transactional listener is outcome oriented and approaches conversations in a linear, sequential way. It's a strong approach for getting things done. It usually doesn't damage relationships and, when applied well, can help build them because it helps people get their most obvious needs addressed. It can be the listening style of choice in a range of situations. Particularly at work, if you and your colleagues are all in an overworked and overwhelmed state, the efficiency of the transactional style can be greatly appreciated. If it's the only style you use, however, you'll end up leaving relational value on the table.

Profile of a Transformational Listener

If you're a transformational listener, you make connections and help others make them as well. You make connections between ideas, and more important, you establish connections between and with other people. The result of transformational listening is coming out of the conversation with more than either of you imagined or hoped for. For Per Wingerup of CBS, the sign of a transformational conversation is when both parties leave thinking, "Wow, that was a great conversation. There were a lot of aha!s. I feel really good about myself leaving that conversation." In his experience, that outcome requires

> really getting down to the heart of the matter and having a real conversation, a vulnerable conversation where you can talk about your threats and your concerns and what you're not sure about. . . . I don't have answers to questions that come up nine out of 10 times. I have no idea, no clue. I know how to go and figure it out, but in the moment, I don't know. If I have to take myself seriously and say, "Either fake an answer or feel too self-assured," it's not a good ingredient for a good conversation. I think "Don't take yourself so seriously," for me, really speaks the truth.

Tracy Columbus, the personal manager we met earlier in the book, has a great way of describing her approach to transformational listening:

> When I have a beginner's mind during parts of my day, learn something new, listen more intently, listening not with a goal of getting something out of it but truly listening to what people are sharing, other people feel it.

When you practice transformational listening, you use more than your ears. You use your eyes to observe the unspoken messages the other person is sending and to convey that you understand what they're saying. You're also not afraid to use silence because you understand that sometimes the best ideas or most important insights require time to form. You intuitively know what Ram Dass meant when he wrote, "The quieter you become, the more you can hear." You understand the importance of the question that Robert Greenleaf, author of the classic *Servant Leadership,* asks in this passage from his book:

> A relaxed approach to dialogue will include the welcoming of some silence. It is often a devastating question to ask oneself, but it is sometimes important to ask it—"In saying what I have in mind will I really improve on the silence?"[3]

As Dinabandhu Sarley shared with me, a fully applied approach to transformational listening can create larger possibilities:

> On a deeply personal level, I actually try to create a resonant field between me and the people I'm with that brings out their best, diminishes their fear, encourages their courage, and opens collaborative possibilities for us. . . . That's what I'm mainly doing. The rest of the stuff is all bric-a-brac around that.

Transformational listening is what you demonstrate when you're fully present and attentive during a meeting or conversation. If mindfulness is the demonstration of awareness and intention, transformational listening is the mindfulness alternative in action.

Other Relational Routines That Build Connection

Of course, other relational routines besides listening can reinforce how you are at your best and help you create the outcomes that are most important at home, at work, and in the community. What just about all of them have in common is that they require an investment of time. That can be a challenge if you're already feeling overworked and over-whelmed. As you consider which relational routines are important to include in your Life GPS, also consider the potential return on the time you invest. Part of that calculus will include your point of view on relationships—are they a means to an end or an end in themselves? Perhaps they're both. As we've already discussed, strong relational ties can support your results over the long run as well as your personal health and well-being. They can definitely help you show up at your best and, in that sense, are a means to an end. Strong relationships can also help you help others show up at their best. In that sense, it seems, strong relationships move from means to an end to ends in themselves.

With that in mind, here's an overview of relational routines that have worked for a number of people I've coached or have interviewed for this book. There's a lot here. Some will resonate with you; some won't. They may spark ideas for you on one or two relational routines that you want to implement that are relatively easy to do and likely to make a difference for you and the people in your life. For ease of use, the ideas and stories that illustrate them are organized by the category of people the routines focus on. Think of them as a series of Habit Hacks for the relational domain.

Yourself

Do you say things to yourself that you would never say to someone you care about? Most of us do from time to time—some of us more than others.

We chastise ourselves when we don't live up to our own expectations. We berate ourselves when we make a mistake. We kick ourselves when we forget something important. It all adds up to mental chatter and clutter that keeps us from showing up at our best. It definitely affects the quality of our relationships with others. As a friend of mine said to me once, "You never meet anybody but yourself."

Here's why it's important to establish a relational routine with yourself.

Your thoughts control your feelings. Your feelings lead to your actions. Your actions determine your results. If your thought monologue about your own performance is consistently negative, you're going to end up feeling pretty bad about yourself, and that's going to affect the quality of your relationships with others.

A self-relational routine I recommend to my clients is inspired by the big idea from Ken Blanchard and Spencer Johnson's classic book, *The One Minute Manager*—"Catch 'em doing something right."

When you observe that your self-talk is mainly critical, stop and ask yourself, "What's going right?" Great; that's one thing. What else is going right? I'll practically guarantee you there is more than one thing. Establish the relational routine of asking and building on the question "What's going right?"

Life Partners

If you're in a marriage or other committed relationship with a life partner, you know that its health and vibrancy depends on investing time in it. That can be challenging in an overworked and overwhelmed world. Sometimes it requires coming up with out-side-the-box solutions. As an example, Keith and Suzan Bickel had a brainstorm 15 years ago that led to a weekly tradition that is relatively easy to do and has definitely made a difference in their marriage.

Keith is a public policy expert in one of the world's largest banks. Suzan runs the Food and Drug Administration practice as a senior partner in a high-powered law firm. Even with such demanding jobs, Keith and Suzan have made spending time and experiencing life together an important priority in over 25 years of marriage. For the first 10 years of their marriage, it was just the two of them and it was relatively easy to carve out some regular time together. Then, with the arrival of a baby daughter, life was more joyful but also more complicated. As Keith described it to me, as their daughter became a toddler they were "burning the candle at both ends and in the middle." The demands of parenting combined with their jobs left very little time to connect with each other. Even when they had time for a date, they often couldn't find a babysitter. Then they realized that they could take advantage of their daughter's time at day care. They set a standing date with each other for lunch on Wednesdays. A few years ago, to accommodate commuting schedules, they changed the date from Wednesday lunches to breakfast bagels on Friday. The only rule they have for their weekly dates is they can talk about anything—travel, movies, friends, goals, challenges—except their daughter. She's an enormous blessing and focus of their lives; she's just not the topic of the Friday breakfast conversation. When I asked Suzanne to give me the headline on what the benefit of having a weekly lunch or breakfast together for 50 weeks of every year for the past 15 has been, she answered, "I can put it in a word: *connectedness.*"

Children

If you're a parent, you might be able to relate to the title of a book about modern parenting by Jennifer Senior called *All Joy and No*

Fun. Kids can be a great source of joy in your life, and they can also be a source of stress and guilt as you try to juggle all of the commitments you have in addition to being a parent. To the degree possible, you may want to consider emphasizing quality of time more than quantity of time. As Evolent Health CEO Frank Williams noted to me:

> We don't have enough time in the day. At some point I recognized that if I spend three fully present hours with my kids that's better than 12 hours with them where I'm not fully present. It's more personally fulfilling for all of us. You get so much more out of it.

Sometimes your children will help you out with that. Back when the BlackBerry was the device of choice, I used to use a picture from a *Wall Street Journal* article titled "BlackBerry Orphans" to start group discussions on how addicted many professionals were to their mobile e-mail device. The picture was a great drawing of a little girl with pigtails angrily throwing the closet doors open to find her guilty dad crouched, hiding and checking his e-mails. One day, I shared the picture with a small group of corporate managers, and one of the guys in the group immediately got this "I'm busted" look on his face. When I asked him what he was thinking, he said, "That happened to me last year."

Being a good sport, he shared with the group the story of how he and his family were making a connection in the Miami airport on their way to a Caribbean vacation. As they were waiting on their flight, his 10-year-old daughter asked, "Daddy, can I see your BlackBerry?" Thinking that she wanted to play a game on it, he said sure and handed it over. She then opened up the zippered pocket on the end of her duffel bag, stuck the BlackBerry in it, zipped it up, and said, "You can have that when we get back, Daddy."

When the corporate guy shared what his daughter did, the whole group pretty much asked at once, "Whoa, what did you do?"

"For the first few minutes, I panicked and debated my options," he replied. "Then, I thought, 'Okay, let me just give this a try one day at a time.' I never asked for it back that week and had the greatest vacation with my wife and kids that I had ever had. When we connected through Miami again on the way home, she took it out of her bag and gave it back to me."

The importance and impact of giving undivided presence and attention to your kids was beautifully illustrated in a story that Elaine Hall shared with me. You may remember from earlier in the book that Elaine is the mother of a son with autism named Neal and that, based on the lessons she learned as Neal's mom, she founded the Miracle Project, an organization that gets children with autism and their families engaged in the arts. In raising Neal, Elaine learned that to connect with him she needed to give herself over to his interests and his timing.

Habit Hack
You're the Boss of Me

When you've been racked and stacked with work meetings all day, it can be hard to make the shift and be present when you walk in the door of your home in the evening. A few years ago, *Harvard Business Review* blogger Peter Bregman shared an idea that might work for you when the kids are ready for you but your mind hasn't quite arrived home yet. When you walk in, set the timer on your smartphone for 10 minutes, hand it to them, and say, "For the next 10 minutes, you're the boss of me!" You might end up getting your kids a cookie (not too many before dinner), playing school, or doing anything else they dream up. You get to shift gears and have some fun, and they get your undivided presence and attention.

She shared this story of the moment when that truth became apparent to her:

> Whenever I joined him inside his world, we would have a connection and his world was just profound. The more I would get into that world of autism, the more extraordinary, beautiful, and vivid it was—a true Zen scape. I remember there was a time where I wanted to take a walk with him and he wouldn't go on the walk with me. He had to stop at every single hubcap, and I would pull him and be like, "Come on, we've got to get going. We've got lots to do; let's just keep going," and he would just have me stop at every hubcap of every single car.
>
> Finally, one day I stopped and looked at a hubcap with him and what I saw was this kaleidoscope of light reflecting from the sun into the hubcap and I shared that with him. I said "Wow, Neal, that is just magnificent. It's so beautiful. Thank you so much for sharing that with me," and he just nodded and from that moment on, we never had to stop to look at hubcaps again.

Some days, you'll have time to stop and smell the roses or look at the hubcaps with your child, and other days you won't. When you don't, it's a good idea to be aware and intentional with yourself and your child about how you feel. Caralyn Brace is vice president and general manager for a nationwide business unit of Unisys. Her job requires a lot of travel and long days. Being able to work from home when she's not on the road helps somewhat, but there's still a lot on her plate. Brace and her husband have a young daughter, so there are a lot of instances in which she has to bring time with her daughter to a close and go to work. She told me that she's very careful in how she frames those moments of transition from playtime to work time:

> Someone once said that the biggest mistake women make in trying to run their career and their families is they apologize all the time and from the day my daughter is born I have never ever said to her I am sorry I have to work, because I am not.

I choose to work, and so I say to her things like, "I am sorry you are sad," or "I sure will miss you," but I never apologize for working.

Family

A big theme I've heard in my interviews for this book is the importance of establishing traditions that become relational routines for one's immediate or extended family. Elizabeth Bolgiano, chief human resources officer of AMAG Pharmaceuticals, shared with me how one tradition helps keep her family connected:

> We're big on building traditions because we've moved around so much in our lives. One of them is going to a particular camp in the Adirondacks every summer, and we've been faithful about doing that. It's a very basic camp. There's no TV. There's no Internet. There's no electronics. It's hiking and being out in nature. While it's an annual routine, it is still something that is a time when we can be together.

And, of course, holidays can be opportunities to build family relationships. The way Melissa McLean Jory describes her family's Thanksgiving tradition may resonate with you:

> We just have a big group of family and people around our dining room table. We have a blast and everybody helps. It's just a celebration of food and love and being together, even with the quirky and strange aunt or whatever. We all have those. . . . It's still a celebration of life and food and appreciation.

Of course, there are the everyday family routines that have nothing to do with traditions or holidays. For instance, several people I talked with for this book mentioned that they make an effort to be mindful—aware and intentional—about spending a little more time on the phone when they make their regular call to their parents—again, easy to do and likely to make a difference, especially to your mom.

Friends

The pace of professional life can make it difficult to stay connected with friends. One way to do that is to make time with friends one of the big rocks you schedule first on your calendar. In doing this, though, there's the question of how wide do you cast your net in giving time to relationships? Your answer will probably be determined in part by your personality—are you more introverted or more extroverted in terms of the energy you derive from connecting with other people? For instance, Susan Cain, the author of the best-selling *Quiet: The Power of Introverts in a World That Can't Stop Talking*, told me:

> I spend like 80 or more percent of my time with probably 10 percent of the people in my world. I think for me that feels right. I'd rather go deeper than go wider. I've had other stages of my life before I was married and had children where I had a really different approach. It was more going out every night and being with lots of different people. I think you have to really tailor your social energy to your life's needs.

Another best-selling author, Wharton's Adam Grant, is on the other end of the spectrum in terms of how he allocates his relational time. For the past few years, he has made it a routine to "reconnect with at least one dormant tie every month":

> I find that when I reactivate an old connection, it's usually the case that we got busy, somebody moved or changed jobs, and we had no desire to fall out of touch. We both walk away really feeling like we've rekindled a relationship, which is fun and intrinsically meaningful.

> It's also, in the creativity sense, beneficial because we've both seen and learned different things since we last connected. It feels like a bigger step forward in a relationship than talking to the people you always talk to because you have a lot to catch up on if you haven't talked to somebody in five years. I love that.

Similar to Grant's dormant ties routine, a client of mine maintains a routine on the way home from work most days of calling one of the 200 or so friends in her iPhone directory just to catch up. That helps her make sure that she's touching base with each of those folks at least once a year. Evolent Health CEO Frank Williams leverages his downtime by making sure that he schedules a meal or a drink with friends who live in the cities he travels to for business. Johnson & Johnson's Lynn Pendergrass keeps her relationships with longtime friends strong by viewing herself as "the ringleader" of her "tribe" and, as such, she is often the one who schedules trips and get-togethers for the group.

Not all relational routines require an extrovert's energy for things like going to dinner, calling friends on the way home from work, or organizing trips for your tribe. Especially in the digital age we live in, a handwritten note or card to a friend can make a difference that you may not even be aware of. Using an example from my own recent experience, I took a few minutes one day to write a note of condolence to an acquaintance whose mother had passed away. I will confess that this is not something I do regularly, but something I read about her mom online inspired me to do so. Months later, this woman was in the conference audience for a presentation I was giving on the content of this book. A few days later she sent me a note that read in part:

> As I reviewed my notes and thought about your own organizing principle of adopting routines (easy to do, and makes a difference), it struck me that 17 months ago, I was the beneficiary of one of your routines. The handwritten note you wrote to me after my mother's death meant so much to me (made a difference to me in my time of sorrow), that you would take the time to write (easy to do). That vivid example of you embodying your own organizing principle will stay with me for years.

Needless to say, her note touched me deeply and has motivated me to keep up a routine of writing personal notes. You rarely learn the nature of the difference that small kindnesses make to other people. I was very fortunate to learn how they do in this case. All of us have multiple opportunities a week to spend a few minutes connecting or reconnecting with friends if we stay open to them.

Colleagues

Given the amount of time we spend at work and the contribution strong relationships make to achieving results, to our overall health and well-being, and to humanity in general, it just makes sense to have relational routines that build connections with colleagues. There are lots of options in this space.

At the most basic end of the spectrum is to get into the habit of responding to people when they reach out to you. As Helen Frye, a senior vice president in a large financial services company, told me, it's easy to say to yourself, "'That's something small. I'll get to it when I get to it,' but to that person it is something big." Establishing a routine of responsiveness—even if it's just to say, "I got your message and will get back with you later in the week," is a classic example of treating others the way you'd like to be treated yourself.

If you're a designated leader in your organization, your relational routines (or lack of them) have a lot of leverage. I'm a big believer in the idea that leaders control the weather. In other words, however you show up as a leader is going to have a big impact on the overall climate in your organization. If you've ever worked in an office where the first question people ask each other in the morning is, "What kind of mood is he in today?" then you know what I'm talking about. Helen Frye is a senior leader who understands the impact she has and makes the most of it through her relational routines:

> One of my little tricks is one I don't admit to many people. When I really don't have a lot of time, I go down and stand in the lobby of the building at lunchtime because a lot of people go out to lunch. I'll stand there like I am waiting to go out to lunch with somebody. Sometimes I sit down just to say hi to people and to connect with them.

No matter what role you play in your organization, consider adopting some routines that establish true friendships with colleagues at work. As well-known research from the Gallup organization tells us, people who have at least one friend at the office are, on average, seven times more engaged in their work.[4] Based on research she conducted for her book *The Progress Principle*, Harvard Business School professor Teresa Amabile described for me the benefits of establishing relational routines that nurture friendships at work:

> You will be able to share things with each other that have to do with the nonwork life. You'll be able to help each other maybe see bright spots in the workday, either moments of beauty, moments of grace, moments of humor, or moments of kindness.

Beauty, grace, humor, kindness—who among us couldn't benefit from more of all of that? They're the qualities that make life worth living. Strong and vibrant relationships with others—at home, at work, and in the community—make it much more likely that we'll experience the sweetness that life has to offer. By establishing relational routines that prompt us to give our time to others, we make life richer and reduce the impact of the factors that lead to feeling overworked and overwhelmed. Relational routines are another key component of the mindfulness alternative.

Coach's Corner

- What style of listening—transient, transactional, or transformational—do you practice most often? What's the impact of that?

- What's one routine in the relational domain that you're not doing now that you think would make the biggest difference to you showing up at your best?

- What person or group—yourself, partner, kids, family, friends, colleagues—could use more of your time and attention? What would that look like in the coming month?

11 What's Your Purpose Here, Anyway?

The Spiritual Routines That Build Perspective

"Dr. Zwiebel Wanted to Meet You"

As the founder and CEO of the fast casual dining leader Panera Bread, Ron Shaich spends a lot of time traveling around the United States visiting with associates and customers of the company's almost 1,800 stores. As he goes from city to city, Shaich hears a lot of comments

---

What You'll Learn in This Chapter

- The two big questions that spiritual routines help you answer

- Five different methods for using the Killer App of the spiritual domain of routines

- Easy to do, likely to make a difference next step ideas for each method

---

about how Panera's restaurants are a gathering place for the people in their communities:

"We're city officials here. We meet here every morning."

"This is our community center."

"This is where I wrote my novel."

"This is where my Bible group meets."

"This is where we moms get together on Tuesday nights to talk and knit."

Shaich loves hearing what Panera means to its customers, but none of the stories he's heard has stuck with him like the one he heard from Dr. Zwiebel. Here's how Shaich remembers it:

> I got to the store, and one of my managers came running up and said, "I'm just so sad. You just missed Dr. Zwiebel and he really wanted to meet you. Would you call him?"
>
> So I called Dr. Zwiebel, and he said, "Listen, I'm 87 years old. I was on the 1952 U.S. Olympic team. I was a psychiatrist in the U.S. Army. I was happily married for 58 years. Four years ago, my wife died. I was just as profoundly sad as any human being could be. Six months after she died, I chose to take my own life. I walked into your Panera store the morning I'd chosen to do it, and the woman behind the counter started flirting with me the way you play with an older gentleman. It made me smile."
>
> He said, "I thought to myself, 'Do I really want to do this? Is there more life left in me?'" He told me, "I've been coming back to this Panera and talking to these people every day for the last four years. I just want you to know something. Your people, your company saved my life."

It probably goes without saying that Shaich was, as he told me, "blown away" by Dr. Zwiebel's story. He also told me that it compelled him to revisit the question of "Why am I here?" At one level for Shaich that was a question about why he's spent more than 25 years building Panera Bread. From that perspective, his answer is, "I'm here because it's the most proper way I know to make a difference." From a larger perspective, his answer has been shaped by the experience of the deaths of his mother, his father, and an uncle he personally took care of for the last three months of his life. As Shaich told me in a conversation recounting those experiences:

> I noticed each time that if you have the time in what is sort of the last out of the ninth inning, you reflect back on your life and you ask yourself, "What do you respect and what don't you?"
>
> My whole view of life is that ultimately the most powerfully informing thing is to bring the future backward, it's future back. I want to ask the question, not in the third out of the ninth inning, but now, "What is it that I respect?" When I stay focused on that, it allows me to ignore, in some way, a lot of the noise.
>
> There's so much chatter in our society that you often lose the signal. You lose what's really important. . . . The way I try to think about my company is the way I think about my life, and I think about them in the same kind of way. What I try to think about is what am I going to respect in 10 or 20 years when I look back on my life? What's going to matter if I could write my own obituary 20 or 30 years from now, and what am I going to feel? . . . I promise you, 100 years from now Panera Bread will be sand. That's not what it's about; this is just the place where I play. To me, play is rooted in doing things I respect.

My conversation with Ron Shaich tees up what I want to talk about in this chapter—the spiritual routines that help you identify and stay connected with the larger purpose of your life.

Discerning Your Purpose

What do we mean when we use the word spiritual? It's a word that means a lot of things to a lot of people. I'll offer an answer that I think cuts across different traditions and perspectives. It's about your life's purpose. Earlier in this book, I suggested that two questions, "What are you trying to do?" and "How do you need to show up to do that?" were very useful in preparing yourself for important meetings, conversations, or events. As it turns out, those two questions in their biggest possible sense are spiritual questions as well. What's the purpose in your life that informs what you're trying to do at home, at work, and in your community, and how do you need to show up at your best to make those outcomes more likely?

When you have routines that keep you connected to your answers to those questions, they help you realize that what you don't want written in your obituary or said at your funeral is what Arianna Huffington jokes about in her speeches—"His PowerPoint slides were always world class," or "Her budget reports were consistently flawless." When you're stuck in a state of chronic fight or flight, it's difficult to keep your perspective focused on the bigger picture. In a state of overwork and overwhelm, those PowerPoint slides or budget reports can seem like the most important thing but they're not. That's not to say that work is not important. It can be and often is, but what is the larger purpose of it for you? What are you really trying to do there? The same question applies to your life at home—what are you really trying to do there? How about in the community where you live: What are you trying to do there?

Spiritual routines can help you get clear about the answers to those "What are you trying to do?" questions and remind you of how you need to show up to make following through on your answers more likely. Your spiritual routines can be religious or nonreligious; many different traditions and perspectives can inform your approach. One of the most helpful perspectives I've heard on what spiritual routines are all about comes from my friend, educator Ward Mailliard. In his point of view, they're about discernment; discerning who you are and what you're about.

In Eastern traditions, that process might be called discerning your dharma. In Western traditions, it might be referred to as following your calling in the sense that the Latin root of the word *vocation* means "to call." Discerning it for yourself might look a lot like what the theologian Frederick Buechner meant when he wrote, "Your vocation in life is where your greatest joy meets the world's greatest need." For Ron Shaich, that looks like the "play" he engages in through Panera Bread. Your answer will be uniquely yours. Spiritual routines can help you determine, in the biggest sense of the questions, what you're trying to do and how you need to show up to do that.

The Killer App of Spiritual Routines: Reflection

While there is certainly more than one way to do it, reflection is the Killer App of spiritual routines. Routines of reflection help create the space for you to be present with your thoughts in a way that ties back to our working definition of *mindfulness*—an awareness of what's going on in and around you that leads to intentional action. You may have noticed that when you're in the overworked and overwhelmed mode, you spend most of your time talking—either to yourself or others. Reflection is more about listening and noticing. It's more about reception than transmission.

The purpose of reflective routines is to slow down your mind enough to notice what's going on with your thinking and your actions. They are routines that help you be still and silent long enough to do that. Stillness and silence can open up the space for insights and perspective on what you're here to do and how you're showing up to do that. Observation and reflection on those two questions without expecting answers or specific outcomes can help strengthen the mental muscles that help you be more responsive and less reactive.

In the rest of this chapter, we'll take a look at five routines of reflection that you might consider as part of your Life GPS and mindfulness alternative. This is certainly not an exhaustive overview of all of your options for spiritual routines or even for those that are specifically routines of reflection. They're simply routines that have worked for others and may work for you. As you consider them, be open to ways that you can modify or adapt any of them to meet you where you are on your own journey. As with routines from any other domain, you don't want to overload yourself. Less is more; better to start with one simple routine that will make a difference for you rather than taking on one or more that are not good fits. Doing that would just make you anxious or self-critical and spin up the fight or flight response that you're trying to mitigate in the first place. We'll start with two routines that are relatively easy to do at any time of the day and conclude with three more that may work best for you on a regular schedule but can also come into play throughout the day. Again, don't pick all five at once. Start with one.

Taking Time for Gratitude

Kaye Foster Cheek, a longtime senior executive, has a wake-up routine that reminds her that she's just happy to be here. She says that while she used to jump right out of bed and check her e-mail, she doesn't do that anymore:

> I open my eyes and before I get out of bed, the first thing I do is say, "Phew, another day. What a gift. Thank you for this breath." For me it starts with the breath. The fact that I open my eyes and I am breathing starts my day with gratitude. I just say thank you for the breath and I am conscious of literally the intake of breath through my nostrils and out through my mouth.

That routine of gratitude sets Foster Cheek up for the rest of the day. After her expression of thanks for another day of life, she thinks about how she wants "to show up that day."

Alanson Van Fleet, the financial services executive who starts each morning with his happy hour, takes his first moment of gratitude when he walks into his office each morning. A little Buddha statue on his desk reminds him to be thankful that someone is paying for "this space, someone has bought the computer, someone is paying for the lights. . . . I feel so grateful and privileged and I recognize that every day. I open up my heart and my mind and I ask myself to make sure I do my best this day."

In the midst of an overworked and overwhelmed state, it's easy to overlook all the things in your life there are to be grateful for. Just being in good enough health to get out of bed and go to an office where you have a job is a great place to start. All too often, however, the extrinsic interference that naturally emerges in life can create that intrinsic fight or flight response that can make you think nothing is going right. You can counteract that by adopting a routine of taking a deep breath and a few moments to ask yourself throughout the day, "What *is* going right?" In other words, what are you grateful for?

Can't come up with good answers to that question? Start by running through the thoughts generated by considering the four domains of routines—physical, mental, relational, and spiritual. What's in your life in any of those four domains that you're grateful for? Then move on to the three arenas of life—home, work, and community. What's in your life in any of those arenas—tangible or intangible—that presses your gratitude button? In any of those domains or arenas, don't just limit yourself to what's happening now. What has already happened in your life that you feel grateful for? How did those things happen? Who was responsible for that? As Steve Jobs said in the

*Habit Hack
Guided Gratitude
Meditation*

Sometimes it can be helpful to have someone lead you through a gratitude meditation. The verbal cues and pacing can help you relax and open up your heart and mind. If you'd like to experience a five-minute gratitude meditation, check out the one I've recorded for you that's available on the video page of ootma .eblingroup.com

legendary commencement speech he gave at Stanford University in 2005 (watch it on YouTube if you haven't seen it), you can't connect the dots prospectively; you can only connect them retrospectively. When you connect the dots that led you to this place, who are the people in your life who helped generate the good fortune and blessings you've experienced that enabled you to be here today?

Next Steps on Taking Time for Gratitude

If all of that feels good and maybe even overwhelming in a good way, don't let it be a one-time thing. Consider making time for gratitude a regular routine of reflection. The next time you find yourself in a fight or flight state of "This sucks," take some deep breaths to activate your mindfulness alternative and ask yourself, "Okay, what's going right? What am I grateful for?"

Want to go deeper with gratitude? Check out the guided gratitude meditation I'm offering in the accompanying Habit Hack.

Centering through Visual Focal Points

Another way to activate your sense of gratitude is to just look around the space you're in. It is likely that there are visual cues or focal points that will remind you of what you're grateful for. Or it may be that you have focal points that help you center and reflect on what you're here to do and how you're showing up for that purpose.

For personal manager Tracy Columbus, Southwestern art is a visual focal point. She once had the opportunity to represent a cofounder of the American Indian movement, and he introduced her to Southwestern and American Indian artists who create images that she says, "just touch my soul." She explained to me:

> In my office, I have several images that just open my mind and heart. It's important for me to be able to know that I can look at those things if I am feeling a sense of dis-ease. . . . They're very simple tools that help me disconnect from that which causes dis-ease and reconnect through things, images, colors, or quotes that bring me joy, energy, and a sense of purpose.

Art is also a visual focal point for veteran author and consultant Peter Block:

> When I walk in a room in which I'm surrounded by art that means something to me or represents something to me, I think, "Somebody stood in front of this canvas for a long period of time and had the patience to make this and create this art." It just calms me down. Art has that effect on me.

As mentioned earlier, Alanson Van Fleet keeps a little Buddha statue on his desk. It's just one of a number of things grouped together in his workspace that have meaning for him and that serve as triggers for reflection during the day. He sent me a picture of the Buddha and the other objects on his desk and told me what each of them means to him:

> There's the little Buddha that's about an inch and a half tall. Next to it is a Canadian coin called a toonie; it reminds me of a friend I have in Canada who led me on (a spiritual) path.

Then there's a little bronze creature that a friend gave to me almost 30 years ago now. It's got a set of scales on its back, and it reminds me that over the years I certainly have grown an armor to protect myself, but that armor also gets in the way of growing, so I pay careful attention to that. Finally, there's a little box from a very special trip I took with our daughter to Mexico one year. It's like a stamp box, I guess. That's what it was designed to hold, but it reminds me of my family. . . . It sits right next to my laptop. It's with me every minute of the workday.

Van Fleet also told me that he tries to schedule his meetings during the day for 45 minutes rather than for an hour in length so he can have a little bit of reset time each hour. During those 15 minutes to himself, he takes two or three minutes to focus on one of those four items on his desk "just to kind of bring myself into a centered spot."

Next Steps for Centering through Visual Focal Points

Creating or collecting some items that serve as visual focal points that trigger moments of reflection is something that's relatively easy to do and could make a difference for you. Consider giving some thought this week to the visual focal points that would help you connect with those biggest picture questions about what you're here to do and how you're showing up for that purpose.

Reflective Reading

Regularly taking time to read material that inspires you, challenges you, broadens you, or sparks thoughts that help you connect the dots can be a great routine of reflection. For instance, Wharton School professor Adam Grant has a routine of reading a book that's completely unrelated to his work—usually a novel or a biography—right before he goes to bed. He finds that kind of reading opens up a sense of flow in his mind more than almost anything else he does. He told me, "I often wake up with new ideas. The same connections between sorts of ideas that were mentioned in a novel or a particular way of telling a story in the biography that feeds into work that I'm doing the next day." The nighttime reading routine is something Grant looks forward to and the timing works for him when his "plate is cleared" at the end of the day because, as he says, "there's nothing else I could or should be doing . . . (or) that could be commanding my attention."

In contrast to Adam Grant, the former CEO of Burberry and now head of retail for Apple, Angela Ahrendts reads for reflection first thing in the morning. In an interview for a *Fast Company* magazine profile, she shared that she draws a bath early each morning and "spends about half an hour meditating on inspirational books" that range from the poetry of Maya Angelou to the work of management guru Jim Collins to the leadership advice of Christian author John Maxwell. She said that morning reading time in the tub is "my peace. That is my space. The world is moving fast. Unless I can come in in the morning and smile, walk in the lobby and say, 'Good morning!'—if I'm stressed—I am not going to do a good job."[1]

Peter Block sees reading as a "form of meditation" and looks for nonfiction authors that make "so much sense" to him and that remind him of and bring him back to his world view. Community Mercy Health Partners CEO Paul Hiltz reads a lot on leadership and on spirituality. Books are part of his reflective reading routine, but he says:

> There are other ways I do it, too. I try to keep little articles, little snippets out of books that I find to be powerful. I keep those around, and I'll read a little something for only a couple of minutes that is inspirational to me while I'm working. It sort of changes the dynamic a little bit.

Next Steps for Reflective Reading

If you're considering reading as a routine of reflection, I strongly suggest you consider an analog rather than a digital approach to your content to reduce the likelihood that you'll be distracted by all the other ways you can spend your time online. If you use a device like a Kindle or another tablet to do most of your reading, consider putting it in airplane mode while you do your reflective reading. You'll get more out of it because it will be easier for you to be centered and still with what you're reading.

Repetitive Prayer or Meditation

If I had to sum up the point of this entire book in just one word, it would be *breathe.* As we've discussed countless times throughout the book, breathing is such an important starting point for overcoming the chronic fight or flight that leads to feeling overworked and overwhelmed. Taking three deep breaths is a gateway to the mindfulness alternative. For many people, breathing is also the foundation for a mindfulness meditation routine that helps them reduce and manage their stress, strengthen their mind's capacity for awareness and intention, and as we've discussed earlier, even lengthen their lives through meditation's positive effect on gene expression.

All of that is great, but what do you do if you can't focus on your breath for more than a few breaths or a few minutes? That's the case for a lot of people who would benefit from meditation but just can't make the focused breathing thing work for them. The good news is that there are options.

In breathing-based meditation, the breath serves as a rhythmic, repetitive focal point that quiets your mind and helps activate your rest and digest response. That can create the conditions you need for reflection. If you're really wound up with the hormones and neurochemicals that stem from a condition of chronic fight or flight, your breath may not be a strong enough focal point. If that's the case, you could probably benefit from a meditation routine that focuses on a word, phrase, or image that you rhythmically repeat to yourself for five to 20 minutes. Of course, you'll still be thinking about thoughts other than your word, phrase, or image during that time (everyone does), but using something that is a little more tangible than your breath as the focus of the rhythm can make it easier for you to notice when your mind wanders. Once you notice, you simply come back to your repetitive rhythm.

> *Habit Hack*
> *Visualize Your*
> *Breathing*
>
> For a lot of people, just focusing on their breath or a word or phrase is a hard routine to start. If that's the case for you, visualizing an image as part of your repetitive prayer or meditation routine may be easier. In a short segment on the video page of ootma .eblingroup.com, I share with you a breathing visualization routine that I use in my own morning time of reflection. It might be a routine that will work for you, too.

There are routines that you may have learned a long time ago that can help you with this. Repetitive prayer can be one of those routines. It can both calm you down and create space for reflection. A quick example of how comes from Henry Lescault, the detective and federal law enforcement agent we met in Chapter 3. Here, he explains how prayer fits into his routine of just closing his door for 10 minutes during the workday to ground himself for what's ahead:

I do pray. I was raised Catholic, and my mom used to take me to church every weekend. And I love her for that. As part of that 10 minutes, I always end with three or four different prayers and that helps center me.

Repetitive, rhythmic prayer in the form of a "Hail Mary" or "Our Father" and counting rosary beads is an important part of the Catholic tradition that Lescault was raised in. Elizabeth Bolgiano of AMAG Pharmaceuticals also uses repetitive prayer as part of her meditative routines for reflection, as she describes here:

Some days it's five minutes on the floor in the basement after I've worked out, just going through repetitive prayers that are very helpful for me to kind of calm myself and get my breathing into the right place and clear my mind. Then some days it can be two or three times a day for half an hour or more at a time.

Meditative or contemplative prayer is also a part of the reflective routines of Kaye Foster Cheek:

[In the morning it's] brushing my teeth and all the little rituals overlaid with just a thankfulness and gratitude for the ability to do those things. And then I always go to prayer. I am a person of Christian faith, and I have a set of practices that I do [that includes a] 10 minute meditation every morning that's based on contemplative prayer. With the prayer work and reading from the Bible, I have a couple of things that guide me in that first hour of the morning.

Foster Cheek's daily routines of reflection proved particularly vital to her when she worked through a decision to leave a highly visible position in her industry for a situation that was better suited to her. As she told me:

I came to that decision through prayer and Pilates. That really is what happened because the prayer part was really just being completely open to being guided by a force other than myself, my own stubborn willfulness that basically said, "There is no way that I am not going to do this. I am going to do this; I am going to

defeat this," and instead of seeing it as something to be con-
quered, really stepping back and asking, "What is the highest and
best use of myself and the gifts that I've been given?"

There is only so much beating against the wall that you can do,
and I came to the conclusion that my time there had come to its
natural end and I absolutely could have stayed there and continued to kind of pound against the wall, but I wouldn't have been
fulfilled. I wouldn't have been the best parent. I would not have
been my best self.

But I am really serious about prayer and Pilates. Pilates was a
euphemism for the physical strength that was required and a
euphemism not just for prayer but for the silence and for all the
other practices that created enough space for me to have the
humility to make a change.

Of course, your reflective routine of repetitive meditation
doesn't have to focus on prayer. It can focus on a word or short
phrase that means something to you or it can be a word, phrase, or
sound that doesn't necessarily mean anything at all. The point is to
give your mind something to focus on over a period of time other
than your random, discursive thoughts. Again, when you notice that
you're lost in random thought, simply come back to your word or
phrase. The rhythmic repetition of that process will open up space
for reflection. The insights may or may not come during the meditation itself. The purpose is to create the conditions and space in
your mind for the insights whenever they come.

Next Steps for Repetitive Prayer or Meditation

As far as other aspects of how to meditate, do what's comfortable
for you. You can be in a comfortable chair or on the floor with
your legs crossed. Your spine doesn't need to be perfectly straight,
but you want to take a posture that allows you to breathe easily.
It's probably best to not lie down when you pray or meditate as
that makes it too easy to fall asleep. Your eyes can be open or

closed. Your environment doesn't need to be one of total silence but on the quieter side is preferable, especially when you're starting out. Finally, consider downloading a meditation app that has a timer you can set on your smartphone or tablet. That way you won't have to worry about the time, the device will take care of that for you.

Journaling

Keeping a journal of your thoughts and feelings about what goes on in your life and the hopes you have for it is a time-tested routine of reflection. By regularly writing in a journal, you can both create space for reflection as well as capture insights that come from reflection. Historical records show that journaling was practiced in both Asia and the Middle East as far back as the ninth century. More recently, years of research conducted by James Pennebaker and his associates at the University of Texas and elsewhere show that a regular practice of writing in a journal for 20 minutes a day can improve your immune system response, lower your blood pressure, and reduce stress.[2]

In the research she conducted for her book *The Progress Principle*, Harvard Business School professor Teresa Amabile and her coauthor (and husband) Steven Kramer asked 238 employees in seven different companies to keep a diary of their experiences and thoughts during their workday. Inspired by her research work, Amabile began keeping a journal of her own several years ago. When I asked her what difference journaling has made for her, she said:

> It certainly has helped me become more mindful about my work and the place of my work in relation to the rest of my life. I think it's helped me to achieve better balance. It's also helped me to see more meaning in my work, and very fundamentally, it's helped me to keep track of my progress.

Amabile notices that when she journals, she has what she calls "crystal moments" when things "stand out in clear relief" for her:

> Sometimes it's something very small. It could be something beautiful that I saw. It could be something that someone said. It could be something that I did that caused a certain thing to happen, a reaction from someone. Usually it's positive. Sometimes it's negative, but what I do (is ask), "Why are you having the emotional reaction you're having to that event? Why is that meaningful to you? What is that telling you?"

I've kept a journal myself for the better part of the past 15 years and have had benefits similar to those of Professor Amabile's. One of the biggest benefits of journaling for me has come when I occasionally look back on what I've written over the past year or so. Invariably, I am struck by how much progress there's been in different aspects of life. It's often the case that the progress has been so incremental that I wouldn't have recognized it without looking at the historical reference points that I ended up capturing in my journal. The other big aha! for me from looking back on old journal entries is how often the things I was worrying about a year ago are no longer worries in the present day. It's been a great way to recognize that no condition or state is permanent (especially those related to my health) and that significant change is always possible and usually likely.

Amabile told me that she, too, looks back at her journal entries from time to time and, as a result, observes that:

> It's so easy in our overwhelmed, professional lives to lose track of where we're going or the fact that we are going somewhere, that we are actually moving toward some goals, especially on those days that are really frustrating where you feel like you didn't get a chance to focus on your real work, your most important work because things kept coming up. Often you can find that in those things that kept coming up, you actually got some important things done. It may not be

the things that you planned, but you did get something done
that mattered. It's made me more mindful during the day of
these little things that are the small wins, occasionally the big
breakthroughs—actually the very small wins. Journaling has
helped me to have a more balanced view of my life because
I'm not consumed with the frustrations and the things that I
didn't get to do.

Next Steps for Journaling

If journaling is a reflective routine that you're interested in, it's
pretty easy to get started. First, decide whether you want to go
analog or digital with where you write. You might like the tactical
feel of putting pen on paper in a notebook dedicated to your
thoughts. If that's not your thing, consider a word processing
program, a multiplatform note-taking app like Evernote or setting
up a simple blog for yourself online on a platform like Tumblr or
WordPress. The important thing is to have a dedicated place to
write your thoughts. Getting into a routine with a particular time
of day is also helpful in staying consistent. When you sit down to
write, start with whatever comes up first in your mind. Don't judge
what you write; just write. Consider setting a goal for yourself of
filling up a certain number of pages or writing for a certain amount
of time. Doing that will give you more space for reflection in those
moments when the words aren't flowing and you're tempted to just
stop and get out of your seat.

Integrating Your Routines of Reflection

As you experiment with routines of reflection and determine which
ones are most helpful in clarifying what you're trying to do and how
you need to show up to do that, you may decide to integrate some of
them together into a regular routine of reflection. Be forewarned and

okay with the idea, however, that that could take years. On my best days, when I'm not traveling across time zones, getting up early to give a speech or catch a plane, or having an early meeting with a client, my integrated routine looks like this:

After waking up and getting breakfast, I read for 10 or 15 minutes from books on different spiritual traditions. That kind of wakes up my brain and gets me in an open mental space. Then I'll meditate for 20 to 30 minutes. I wrap up with writing one to three pages in my journal while I'm listening to the Mozart channel on Pandora. (There's something about Mozart's music that puts my brain in the right place for journaling.)

I know that sounds like a lot and I guess it is, but that's not where I started. As best as I can remember, when I started my morning routine more than 15 years ago, it was 5 or 10 minutes of reading followed by 5 minutes of journaling. I tried different kinds of prayer and meditation for years until I found the versions that work best for me. (They work for now at least; that could change and probably will. That's cool.) In the past 15 years, I've had months or, in one case, an entire year when I didn't journal at all. I was tired of my own voice and decided to give it a rest during those times. When I'm on the road and waking up at 6:00 AM local time when my body thinks it's 3:00 AM, I adjust to fit the reality of the moment. I might meditate for five minutes on a morning like that with the hope of coming back to more of the routine later in the day.

The point in sharing all of that is to give you a glimpse of how things work for one person and what it looks like under varying circumstances. It's all part of the process. That's actually what we're going to cover in the next short chapter to wrap up this part of the book on the routines that help you show up at your best. What happens when your routines sort of run off the rails, and how do you get things back on track when they do?

Thoughts and answers on those questions and more are in the next chapter.

Coach's Corner

- What's the purpose in your life that informs what you're trying to do at home, at work, and in your community?

- What routines do you currently have to create space for reflecting on your purpose and how you're showing up against that purpose?

- What could you do to take your routine of reflection to the next level?

---

12 Making It Work

Tips for Following Through (And for Rapid Recovery When You Don't)

Your Checklist for Staying on Track

One of the go-to lines that yoga teachers like to use when they're asking the class to do something challenging is, "It's not yoga perfect; it's yoga practice." That's a good metaphor for life actually. We're not here to be perfect; we're here to do the best we can. The same thing goes for the goal of showing up at your best, the routines that help you do that, and the outcomes that you hope your actions will lead to. None of that is going to be perfect. As they say in the military, no plan survives first contact. Life is a process of adjustments.

As we wrap up this discussion on the routines that help you show up at your best, let's spend some time talking about how to follow through on your routines in a way that reduces overwork and

---

What You'll Learn in This Chapter

- How to stay on track with your routines
- Why you should lighten up on yourself
- How to get back on track when things run off the rails

---

overwhelm and reinforces your mindfulness alternative. Because perfection is not the goal, let's also spend some time on a few principles for recovering rapidly when all of those extrinsic factors throw you off your game. Some of what we'll cover is a recap of points we discussed earlier in the book; other points are made for the first time in this chapter. By weaving them together here, my intent is to give you an easy to use checklist of what to do to on both the before and after aspects of keeping the routines in your Life GPS on course.

Before we do any of that, though, let's do a quick reality check. How much pressure do you feel yourself putting on yourself right now? If you feel any, acknowledge that and know that you're not alone. It's not yoga perfect; it's yoga practice. As one of my all-time favorite instructors, Alison, used to say to her class full of Type A, overworked and overwhelmed superachievers, "You guys look so serious! Come on, it's just a freaking yoga pose."

As you approach your routines, keep that in mind—metaphorically speaking—it's just a freaking yoga pose. Yeah, that routine you've undertaken will definitely do some good, but the world's not going to end if you don't follow through for a day, a week, a month or even a year. Sure, if you think it's going to make a difference for you, it's good to get things back on track, but let's agree that you'll hold it all lightly as you do. After all, the point of this is to reduce feeling overworked and overwhelmed and to strengthen the mindfulness alternative, right? Let's not approach the routines with an itty-bitty shitty committee mind-set that just makes things harder, okay?

All good? Great, let's continue. Here's the checklist of tips.

Tips for Following Through on Your Routines

Know Your Performance Patterns and Operating Rhythms

You know that disclaimer they use in television commercials for mutual fund companies—past performance is not a predictor of future performance? That's actually not so true when it comes to following through on your routines. If you've had trouble sticking to routines in the past, you probably will again in the future unless you take a little time to analyze what works best for you in terms of your natural performance patterns and operating rhythms. For instance, if getting up in the morning is a struggle for you, telling yourself that you're going to get up at 5:00 AM everyday for 30 minutes of cardio probably isn't a great strategy for success. Sticking with that example, maybe spending 30 minutes on the treadmill or elliptical machine is your personal idea of hell at any time of the day. It's good to call all of that out in advance and choose accordingly. Maybe a brisk walk during the day would be a better option for you. To take an example from the relational domain of routines, it wouldn't make a lot of sense to say you're going to have dinner with your family five nights a week if you've got a houseful of teenagers and both you and your spouse work outside the home. Maybe going out for brunch on the weekends would work better for you—or not. The point is to take some time to assess and be realistic about your recent performance patterns and operating rhythms when you are selecting routines that will help you show up at your best.

Pick the Routines That Are Easy to Do and Likely to Make a Difference

The reason I've talked about this principle throughout the book is because it's so damn important. As you choose routines for your Life GPS, start with easy ones that will make a difference. There are so many things you could choose to do on a regular basis that are relatively hard to do that would make a difference. The problem is that they won't make a difference because they're too hard for you to either learn how to do or fit into your life. For instance, going to a 90-minute yoga class five days a week would probably make a big difference for you. The problem is you probably can't identify the 10 or so hours a week—at a minimum—it would take to fit in all of those chair poses and downward facing dogs. So, why not start with a 30-minute online class you can do in your living room three times a week? That's still going to make a difference for you but is a lot easier to do. After a month or two of that, add in a class at your gym on Saturday or figure out a way to get to a class at a studio on Tuesday and Thursday nights. Before you know it, you're doing yoga five days a week. It just didn't require an upfront commitment of 10 hours a week. (And, again, I'm not saying you have to do yoga. It's just an example.)

Schedule the Big Rocks First

This is another one that we've talked about a few times already. It bears repeating, though, as you work on setting yourself up for success with your routines. The very word *routine* implies that you're going to do something on a regular basis. If they're actually routines that help you show up at your best and make it more likely that you create the out-comes you're hoping for at home, at work, and in the community, they're big rocks. Schedule them first. To take an example from earlier in the book, Hilton CEO Chris Nassetta schedules dinner with his dad and other family members and friends on Tuesday nights. He's been doing it for 40 years. Does it happen every single Tuesday? Nope, life does have a tendency to intervene, but because the Tuesday dinner is a standing commitment on his calendar, he's compelled to ask if another request for his time is worth missing the big rock of having dinner with his dad. Once you identify the routines that matter most to you, get them on your calendar.

Master Your Inner Monologue

So, getting those big rocks on your calendar is one thing; actually following through on them is another. If you're human (and who here isn't?), you've had times when that inner monologue starts cranking in your head as the calendar notification starts flashing for that commit-ment you made days ago. While the script can vary, the monologue is along the lines of, "Oh, man, I don't feel like doing that at all. Maybe I should just skip it today."

Danae Ringelmann of Indiegogo knows all about that monologue and has observed through the years that when it's telling her to skip something she's committed to doing for her own good, she almost physically feels the urge to not do it. That's become her signal that she needs to suck it up and do it anyway. She first noticed the dynamic in a public speaking course that she signed up for in college. Like a lot of people, the idea of speaking in public made Ringelmann anxious and she regularly had that inner monologue telling her to skip the class because it was just too uncomfortable. She went anyway and, as it turns out, it changed the course of her life. As she told me:

> Public speaking has become one of the critical ways we've grown Indiegogo. We had no marketing power. We had nothing. All we had was ourselves. We had to get out there and talk. It actually became critical for me to learn how to do that. It became critical in our success.
>
> That was kind of the first big lesson. So anytime where I literally have a physical reaction to something, that's my trigger that that means I need to do it.

Recruit Some Buddies

Whenever we run a group coaching program in my company, we always have the participants pair up as peer coaches for the duration of the seven-month program. The expectation is that they spend at least 20 minutes a week—10 minutes in each direction—coaching and encouraging each other to keep going on whatever it is they're working on. When I debrief people on what they get out of that process, one of the most frequent responses is, "I didn't want to show up for my call not having done what I said I was going to do last week, so I went ahead and did it." It's that whole accountable partner thing.

You can and probably should use the same principle to help you follow through on your most important routines. Recruit some buddies to be your coaches and accountability partners. Tell them what you're working on and ask them to ask you how it's going on a regular basis. Better yet, ask them to join you in the routine. On the relational routines front, for example, it's hard to have a date night by yourself. On the physical routines, you're a lot less likely to skip the workout or the class if you know that a friend is there waiting on you. On the spiritual routines, it can be really meaningful to share what you're doing and learning with a friend or family member who's on a similar path.

Ask for Feedback

As you recruit some buddies, give them permission to give you feedback on the routines you're engaging in for which they have line of sight. When you do, you may want to give them a guideline that was first proposed by the Apostle Paul: "Speak the truth in love." In other words, ask them to keep it real while holding your best interests at heart. When I was interviewing her for this book, Kaye Foster Cheek had a great line about how she thinks about the value of feedback from family, friends, and colleagues: "You know, I am human, so there are days when, as my son would say, 'I need my posse to straighten me out.'" Make sure you have some good buddies in your posse who will give it to you straight.

Review Your Life GPS Weekly

If you haven't already downloaded a copy of the Life GPS worksheet from ootma.eblingroup.com, now is a great time to do that. We've already had some extended conversation about determining how you are at your best and, in this part of the book, the physical, mental, relational, and spiritual routines you want in your life to reinforce that. In the next chapter, we'll talk about the outcomes you're hoping to gain by showing up at your mindful best more often. You'll stand a much better chance of staying true to your intentions if you capture your thoughts on a single piece of paper. The Life GPS worksheet is designed to help you do that.

Once you have your answers to the three big components—how you are at your best, the routines that reinforce that, and the outcomes that you hope for—written down, your Life GPS becomes much like the GPS app on your smartphone or the one in your car. Once you enter a destination in the GPS device, you have a much better chance of getting there. When you make a wrong turn in your car, the GPS is able to adjust the route for you because you've already entered where you want to go into the device. Do the same thing with your Life GPS; write down where you want to go and then regularly assess your progress. My recommendation is that you keep your completed Life GPS nearby—at your desk, in your planner, on a bedside table, or in a PDF reader on your tablet are all good candidates—so it's easy for you to glance at it once or twice a day. On a weekly basis, I recommend taking 10 or 15 minutes of reflection time to pull out your Life GPS, look over each of the three main components, and ask yourself, "How am I doing?" If you're like me, you'll probably identify a number of things that you need to adjust in any given week. Pick one or two adjustments to make that are—you guessed it—relatively easy to do and likely to make a difference. Save any other potential adjustments you might make for later. A weekly quick and easy review of your Life GPS can help you stay focused on your mindfulness alternative.

Celebrate Your Wins

We've heard several times from Teresa Amabile, Harvard Business School professor and coauthor of *The Progress Principle.* The focus of Amabile's book and work is the factors that keep people engaged with their work. The primary finding of her research is that if they recognize even one thing each day that they accomplish on something that matters, most people stay motivated and engaged.

The same principle applies to you. As you follow through on your routines, take just a little bit of time to acknowledge your efforts and whatever progress you're making. I know from experience that sometimes it seems like you're not making any progress at all. It can feel like all effort and no progress, and, then, seemingly out of nowhere, you have a breakthrough. It wasn't out of nowhere of course—you were putting in the road miles that made that breakthrough possible. John Rawlinson, the former actor and model who made a career shift to bring integrated wellness practices to hospice patients and their families, shared a Latin phrase with me that describes this process: *festina lente,* which translates as "make haste slowly." You keep at it and keep at it until you see progress. Then you still keep going. Give yourself credit for both the effort and the eventual outcome. Celebrate all of your wins.

Tips for Getting Back on Track

The best coaching question I was ever asked was when I was still an energy company vice president. In a conversation with an executive coach named Deborah Dickerson, I was in the midst of beating myself up for a list of things I hadn't done or had done wrong. After listening quietly for several minutes, Deborah asked, "What would it take for you to stop judging yourself?"

That question hit me like a ton of bricks because it cut to the quick of my perfectionism and feeling like I never measured up to my own expectations. I'd like to be able to report that I was immediately transformed by the question and it was all sunshine and roses from there. That wasn't the case, but by raising the question, Deborah succinctly framed something for me to work on for the rest of my life. If you regularly find yourself in a condition of being overworked and overwhelmed, Deborah's question might be a good one for you, too.

Move on to the Next Play

Remember, it's yoga practice, not yoga perfect. The more we can accept the fact that we're not perfect, the easier it is for any of us to do better. Not long after the Seattle Seahawks won the 2014 Super Bowl, I heard an interview with the team's sports psychologist, Michael Gervais. Seahawks head coach Pete Carroll hired Gervais a few years before to, among other things, teach the team how to meditate and do yoga. (Meditation was optional; yoga was mandatory.) In the interview, Gervais talked about the mind-set that Coach Carroll asked him to help instill in the members of the team. It was all about moments. Even world-class athletes have moments in a game where they blow a play. The goal of Gervais and the Seahawks coaching staff was to help players learn to forget that blown play moment as quickly as possible because the next play could be the game changer, and they needed all of their awareness and intention focused on that moment.

The same principle applies to you when you miss a day, a week, or more of an important routine. When you miss it, let go of the guilt. That doesn't do you any good and just worsens the fight or flight, overworked and overwhelmed feeling. Move on to the next play. Figure out the one or two things you want to do differently tomorrow to get back on track. That doesn't have to be the full-blown routine, by the way. Something—no matter how small—is better than nothing.

Scale Back

There are times in life when you reach a tipping point. Adding one more thing can bring everything crashing down like the last block on the shaky tower in a game of Jenga. The same thing can happen with your routines. Adding one more can totally upset your operating rhythm and create a negative ripple effect across the board. If that happens to you, scale back. Refer back to your Life GPS and remind yourself of the routines that are most clearly in the sweet spot of relatively easy to do and likely to make a difference for you. Regroup by focusing on just that really small number of routines and let yourself off the hook for the others for now. If they're still important down the road, you'll get back to them.

Create Leverage

When it's time to regroup, look for the routines that create the most leverage in your life and double down on those. For instance, if walking is a routine that works for you, keep it because it doesn't just have physical benefits, it also has mental benefits, relational benefits if you share your walks with someone you care about, and even spiritual benefits if it gives you the opportunity for reflection. That's a lot of leverage for an investment of 20 or 30 minutes a day. When you feel like you're off track, look at your routines with leverage in mind. Those are the ones where you want to invest whatever time you have available.

As we wrap up this part of *Overworked and Overwhelmed,* I hope you have some new insights about the routines that will work to help you show up at your best and create the outcomes that matter most to you. Let's continue building your mindfulness alternative by considering what those outcomes might look like and why, while it's important to have an idea of what they are, you'll want to hold the specifics loosely.

Coach's Corner

- What's working for you and not working for you with your operating rhythm? What do you want to keep doing or do differently?

- What are the big rocks in your life that you definitely need to schedule first?

- Who's a buddy that you'd like to invite to be your peer coaching partner in following through on your routines?

Part Four

13 What Are You in It For?

Clarifying Your Outcomes at Home, at Work, and in the Community

Signing Up for Adventures, Large and Small

As is the case with any marriage, when Sian Wayt married Per Wing-erup, she had no way of knowing everything she was signing up for. In her case, one of those things was becoming immersed in her husband's sense of adventure. Growing up as a boy in Sweden, Per's parents scrimped and saved to make sure that their children saw a good part of the world. When he wasn't in school or traveling with his family, Per spent a lot of time running in the woods creating "little adventures."

What You'll Learn in This Chapter

- Why outcomes are important but you shouldn't become too attached to them

- The true connection between actions and results

- How your gifts can make a difference at home, at work, and in the community

---

When they became parents themselves, Sian and Per knew they wanted to pass that sense of adventure on to their children. When their daughters were 10 and 12 years old, they decided to take them out of school for a year to travel around the world. They had talked about it for three or four years and, then, one morning at breakfast looked at each other and said, "Do we want to sit here and have breakfast when we're 65 and the kids are out of the house and say, 'Oh, missed opportunity. Why didn't we do it?'"

"We couldn't afford it, but that didn't matter," Per told me. He resigned from a job that he loved not knowing what he would do for a living after the trip. He and Sian basically took a leap of faith so that, as Per told me, they could teach two important ideas to their kids by going around the world. Per said:

> One, we refuse for them to be afraid of the world. There are so many people who are afraid of so many things. Most things never actually materialize. They're just afraid because they don't know anything about it or it's different. We didn't want the kids to be afraid and the second one was we just want them to know it's not right and it's not wrong. It's just different.

Thanks to Sian's strong talent for logistics and budgeting and her willingness to adopt Per's sense of adventure, the Wingerup family spent nine months visiting 24 countries on six continents. (You can watch a beautiful four-minute video summary of their trip on their blog, familywingerup.com.) As I write this, Per is back in the job he resigned from to take the trip. He didn't know when he left that job would be there for him when he got back.

When I asked him what he learned from this big adventure, Per talked about two things. One was about how much he learned about his preconceived notions from watching the unbiased way his daughters engaged with the world. The other was how important adventures are to him and his family. When I asked him what the last adventure was that he had taken with them, he replied:

> It was yesterday. My youngest daughter had a dance competition in Lowell, which is a town about an hour away from where we live. We never go there. Sian and the youngest went over early and our oldest, Linnea, and I were going over later in the day. We knew where the dance competition was, but we hadn't planned out where we were going to eat or what we were going to see, so on purpose I parked about a mile away from the venue.
>
> We turned off the GPS and I said to Linnea, "Let's just see if we can figure out how to get there. We'll ask locals for help and we'll just venture our way in from here." On the way there we found a great little coffee house where she had the best chai tea latte. If we hadn't gotten lost on purpose on our way there we would've never found this little coffee place. It's just small, little, silly things like that. It doesn't have to be big. I think adventure is more a state of mind.

Actions and Results

The point in opening this chapter with Per's story is not that you should quit your job and travel around the world with your family. The point is to provide some food for thought about the bigger picture outcomes that matter most to you and to give you some space to consider the connection between your actions, the fruits of your actions, and the amount of control you have over both.

The fact is, because all of those extrinsic factors are not in your control, you don't have complete control over your outcomes. That's not to say, however, that you shouldn't consider the kinds of outcomes you hope for in the three big arenas of life: your life at home, your life at work, and your life in the community. You should consider them because having intention around your outcomes will inform and reinforce the actions you take each day. Life isn't a dress rehearsal; this is your one opportunity to create the outcomes that matter most to you at home, work, and in the community. Just don't hold on too tightly to your ideas of what the very specific results of those outcomes should be. Holding tightly to specific notions of how things should be now or will be in the future is the source of a lot of the stress that causes people to feel overworked and overwhelmed. It creates anxiety before you know the outcome and, if things don't go exactly as you planned, disappointment after the outcome. As my wise friend, Ward Mailliard, said to me:

> If you want to be stressed in your life, if that's your goal, be attached to the outcome. . . .
>
> Instead, do the action for its own sake, and don't worry about the results. That doesn't mean you don't care about the results, but you work without worrying about the results. You worry about the quality of what you're doing. You worry about intention.

What Mailliard is talking about is what Gandhi called renouncing the fruit of your actions. In his commentary on the spiritual classic the *Bhagavad Gita,* Gandhi explained it this way:

> Renunciation of the fruit in no way means indifference to the result. In regard to every action one must know the result that is expected to follow, the means thereto, and the capacity for it. He, who, being thus equipped, is without desire for the result, and is yet wholly engrossed in the due fulfillment of the task before him, is said to have renounced the fruits of his action.

When a lot of the programming in the world is about the fruit and not the action, it can be hard to wrap your mind around the idea of renouncing the fruit. For me, a key phrase in that quote from Gandhi is that for "every action one must know the result that is expected to follow." While we should expect outcomes (fruit) from our actions, we shouldn't obsess over them. As we hear so often, it's more about the journey than the destination. As the name of a planning process called the Life GPS implies, direction and a sense of what you're trying to do in the different arenas of your life matters a lot. The premise of the Life GPS is that mindful and high-quality actions (showing up at your best) will lead to mindful and high-quality outcomes. They may not be the exact outcomes you expected at the start, but the likelihood that they will be ones you feel good about is high. Let's spend the rest of this chapter completing your Life GPS by considering the outcomes that matter most to you in the three big arenas of life—home, work, and community—with thoughts sparked by the experience and perspective of some of the people I've talked with about the mindfulness alternative.

Where the Heart Is: Creating Mindful Outcomes at Home

The reason that home is positioned as the first of the three arenas of life is that it's the long-term foundation for everything else you do in life. You may spend a lot of time there or a little, but it's the place you return to at the end of the day. Whether you live on your own, with a friend, with a life partner, or as part of a family, home is your sanctuary. Ideally, it should be that safe place where you and the other people who may live or visit there grow, renew, live, laugh, and love.

When you think about the outcomes you want to create at home, you may think of the space itself. You may have particular ideas about the kind of setting that would nourish and inspire you, your friends, and family.

You may also view home not so much as a place but as a frame of mind that represents aspects of your life or the lives of other people who reside there. Your desired outcomes for home may have a lot to do with the quality of the relationships that the people who live or gather there have with each other. If you live at home with a life partner, you may, like author Susan Piver, think about home as the place where you learn and grow together. What she said when I asked her about her desired outcomes at home may resonate with you if you're in a long-term relationship:

> What's specific for me at home is I'm married; I've been married for 15 years, and that is the best practice anyone ever designed. . . . It's designed to show everything that is ridiculous about you, everything that is wonderful about you, everything that is blind about you, and it's just packed in a nice little package.
>
> So my desired outcome at home is a deepening intimacy with my partner because you can't always expect love and you can't always expect even friendship but you can expect to use everything that happens in your relationship—good, bad, and ugly—as a means to deepen intimacy. That is possible.

Of course, long-term relationships often lead to children, and if you're a parent, a lot of your desired outcomes at home probably focus on the kind of relationship you want with your kids and your hopes for their long-term health and well-being. As a dad of two young adult men myself, I have a lot of appreciation for what Power Yoga creator Bryan Kest observed to me about parenting: "Your children may not listen to you, but they will always become you." Earlier in the book, we talked about how leaders control the weather. If you're a parent, the same holds true for you and your kids. The climate you establish at home will play a big part in whatever outcomes develop for your kids. It reminds me of the story we heard earlier from Godiva Chocolatier CEO Jeri Finard about the moment of truth she had when she was delayed at O'Hare Airport while trying to make it home for an important high school event for her daughter. She made it, but the fear of not getting there in time caused her to reevaluate how what she wanted for her family synced up with what she wanted from her work. It led her to Godiva, where she's been able to stay closer to home while still

pursuing an energetic career. In the process, she believes that the outcomes in one arena have positively affected the other. As she told me:

> I feel like I'm the luckiest person in the world because I was able
> to raise great kids. That has always been my most important proj-
> ect. I always vowed that I did not want to be one of those moms
> where the kids said, "She was there for work and she was there
> for everyone but us." I wanted to make sure that I was there for
> them as well.
>
> I love them, and I also love what I do. I love to work. . . . My hus-
> band has been super supportive. . . . The kids have picked up
> that this is something that I get energy from and that I like. I would
> frankly be quite surprised if my boys ended up with women who
> do not (pursue a career) because that's the only model they have
> known.

Of course, there are a lot of other factors besides your work that
influence outcomes for your kids. One of the big ones on my radar
screen is the influence of what my wife, Diane, and I call competitive
parenting. If you aren't really clear about what you're trying to do for
your kids and why you're trying to do that, it's easy to get sucked into
a dynamic of "they have to do everything that all the other kids are
doing or else they're going to fail at life." When our boys were little, we
used to love to read the Berenstain Bears books to them at bedtime.
The one that made as big an impact on us as it did on them was the
Berenstain Bears in Too Much Pressure. The story was that Brother Bear
and Sister Bear got involved in so many extracurricular activities that
the whole family became overworked and overwhelmed with car pools,
juggling the schedule, missing meals, and the like. It was so bad that
Mama and Papa Bear almost had nervous breakdowns, which made
the kids worried and sad. (Even bears can suffer from chronic fight or
flight apparently.) They regrouped, the kids agreed that they would
each only do two after school activities at any given time, and they all
lived happily ever after. We did our best to follow their example. Our
principle as parents was quality, not quantity, when it came to what

our boys were involved in. My personal opinion is that a lot of parents are stressed because they operate from a position of fear rather than love. They're so afraid that their kids are going to miss out on every possible opportunity that they make themselves and their kids crazy in the process. It's hard to get terrific outcomes when everyone is going nuts.

For most people, the arena of home doesn't just include the nuclear family but also the extended family. As you consider the outcomes you're aiming for at home, you may also consider your parents, siblings, and other relatives as they're all part of the tapestry of your life. It can be helpful to envision the kind of presence you want to exhibit with your family so you'll be prepared when the good and bad times inevitably unfold. For example, a beautiful story I heard in doing the interviews for this book came from John Rawlinson, who described the work that he and his father did together to strengthen their relationship in the last years of his life. Rawlinson's father served as a nuclear submarine commander in the British navy and was the classic, no-nonsense English gentleman. Rawlinson, at that time in his life, had a hectic and exciting career as an international model and actor. When I asked him what his dad's take on his career was, he shared this story with me:

> He did a lot of listening. We worked hard, together the two of us, to try and come to a place of understanding between us. How do I put this? It was patience, I think. There was patience throughout it. I think in a sense, the great thing about being a British gentleman—there are numerous benefits in terms of stoicism and things but they are not great in terms of emotionalism, which is where I came from.
>
> It really was probably not until—actually it was the day before he died. I came back from New York and his eyes lit up and he said, "Oh clever you, you made it." It was nothing, but it just all came out in that one phrase. It was just seeing the look in his eyes and

all that. In many ways, it was the summation of quietly working our way through it together in a truly British *Remains of the Day* kind of way.

One way to nurture the outcomes you're hoping for at home is to, as much as possible, share your life in a way that leaves no regrets. John Rawlinson and his father did the work that enabled them to feel that way.

What Does Success Really Look Like? Creating Mindful Outcomes at Work

In a speech she gave a few years back, Anne Bryant told the job interview story to end all job interview stories. In 1996, she was a finalist to be the executive director of the National School Boards Association. Prior to her onsite interview with the search committee, she did some searching online for stories about the association and mainly found articles about school board members taking "boondoggle" trips and engaging in other questionable behavior. She also found a lot of op-ed pieces from the incumbent executive director, who consistently defended school boards as "the center of democracy."

As the search committee members ended their questioning of Bryant, the chair of the committee asked her if she had any questions for them. Bryant did actually; she related the rest of the story this way:

I asked, "Is this an organization whose mission is to defend school boards as the center of democracy, or is this an organization that wants to make school boards more effective?"

Silence. Nonverbal looks from one to the other and then to Roberta, the chair. She asked me to leave the room! Have you ever been in an interview and been asked to leave the room? I was a bit stunned, took my briefcase, and left. [While I was sitting] out in the hall, the search consultant came by. I said, "Eric, I think I have blown it. Sorry, but you have lots of other candidates right?" He looked very puzzled and mumbled, "You were not supposed to be out for another 20 minutes." As he opened the door to go inside the meeting room, I said, "Oh, would you bring my purse out when you come?" He came back seconds later without my purse and said, "Don't worry, they're talking about your question."

What seemed like 20 minutes was probably 10, and I was invited back in. Standing up to her full 5 foot and 1 inch height, the chair, Roberta, declared, "Anne, we have been discussing your question, and we have an answer. We have *been* an organization that defended school boards; we must *become* an organization that makes school boards more effective!" I was hooked and they never wavered in my 16-plus years with the organization.

With her question, Anne Bryant kicked off the transformation of that organization and its members. Her story frames an important question for you to consider as you think through the outcomes you're hoping for from your work: *What does success really look like?* One way to think about your answer to that question is to consider the range of possible outcomes on a continuum from transactional results to transformational results. There's no judgment here about one end of the spectrum being bad and the other being good. It is just a way to frame up what you're trying to do in your work, how you need to show up to make that likely, and why all of it is important to you in the first place.

By their very nature, outcomes on the far end of the transformational spectrum will require a greater investment of your energy, time, and attention. For example, when Danae Ringelmann cofounded the crowdfunding site Indiegogo, she did it because she wanted to bring personal connection back to finance. That transformative vision is what makes it worth the hours she invests in leading a high-profile start-up. As Pennsylvania's Secretary of Corrections, John Wetzel spends a lot of time on the road speaking because, as he says, "We are trying to not just improve the operation of the department but change legislation and really change how we do corrections. Our goal is to kind of set the example for the country. . . . The country needs it, so it might as well be us." For Jim Campbell, the former CEO of GE Appliances, transformation depended on him showing up as a positive leader with a plan to lead the business through the financial crisis and recession that began in 2008. The energy and focus that Campbell and his team brought to the table led to thousands of GE Appliance jobs coming back to the United States.

Transformational outcomes can be large scale like in the previous examples, or they can be smaller scale results focused on individual people. Your vision may look like that of Rod Swanson, who found that in a decades-long career creating best-selling video games at Electronic Arts, the most meaningful thing he could do was develop other people: "[I found I loved] the idea of if you give them a voice and they feel like you are going to do what they think should be done and then they become responsible for it, you can really change things."

The way you show up at work may be transformative for other people in ways that you may not learn about until much later, if ever. Harvard's Teresa Amabile had that experience. One evening she and her husband were at a Broadway show and were stretching their legs and talking during intermission. A young woman came up the aisle toward her asking, "Dr. Amabile? Dr. Amabile?" The young woman, whose name was Sarah, introduced herself as a student of Amabile's at Brandeis 12 years earlier.

The younger woman was excited to see Amabile again because she wanted to tell her exactly how Amabile changed the course of her life. Amabile was the leader of a weekly psychology lab at Brandeis that included other professors, graduate students, and undergrads. One week Sarah, who was a sophomore at the time, gathered her nerves to offer a suggestion in the meeting. She got a couple of sentences out before a professor cut her off and started talking about her own ideas. As Sarah remembered it, Amabile stepped in and said, "Hold on a minute there. Let's let Sarah finish. Let's hear the rest of her idea." "That's all you did," Sarah said to her. "But it was, to me, a validation that oh, maybe my ideas are actually worth something.

Maybe I can actually do something in this field. . . . The fact that I was a sophomore and you cut off a professor so that I could finish my idea just meant the world to me and I've never forgotten it. That's when I decided I was going to try to pursue psychology as a career."

Amabile told me that as a result of Sarah's story she "was walking on air the rest of that evening and probably the rest of the next day as well."

There are a lot of opportunities to do transformative work. Some require a lot of energy, time, and attention. Others just require being present and attentive in the work you do. Sure, there will always be work that is just transactional by its nature, but don't sell yourself short. As you consider the outcomes you hope to create at work, factor in opportunities for transformation.

Leave It Better Than You Found It: Creating Mindful Outcomes in Your Community

I used to coach an executive named Patrick, who, in addition to his job in a large financial services company, chairs an organization that supports the homeless in his city. Every year, Patrick's organization stages a day in which more than 700 homeless citizens each connect with a volunteer at the city's civic center. The goal is to provide as many essential services to the homeless as possible that day. Stations offering medical and mental health screenings, dental and vision services, barbers and hairdressers, housing assistance, food, and dozens of other services are set up in the civic center. The role of each volunteer is to host and assist a single homeless citizen through their most important stations over the course of the day. It's quite an amazing operation, and I was really impressed when Patrick told me about it. A lot of associates from Patrick's company participate in the program as hosts. When I asked him what people say to him about their experience spending the day helping and getting to know a homeless person, his answer was immediate: "The biggest thing I hear is 'I realized that the person I helped is really not that different from me. They have families; they went to school; they've had jobs. I realize now that if I had made a left turn instead of a right turn somewhere along the way, that could have been me.'"

The most important aspect of Patrick's project is helping people who need help. You could make a strong case, though, that the volunteers get as much from the day as the homeless people they're assisting because it connects them with the life and community beyond their immediate everyday experience. All of us live and work in communities. Some communities are very tangible like the neighborhood, town, or city you live in. Others are based on a common interest like religious faith, profession, hobbies, or other interests. Still other communities are formed around shared challenges such as a medical condition or traumatic experience.

The question to ask when you think about the communities that you are or could be a part of is not only what are you giving to them but also what are you receiving from them? Communities create what Harvard sociologist Robert Putnam calls "social capital," from which everyone involved benefits. As a matter of fact, research conducted by Putnam and his colleagues shows that joining and participating in just one group cuts in half your odds of dying within the next year.[2] My physician, Myles Spar, saw this play out directly when he spent a few years volunteering for Doctors Without Borders. Spar was focusing on stemming the spread of infectious diseases like tuberculosis and HIV in less developed countries. In those years he spent time in a region of the South

Caucasus called Nagorno Karabakh as well as Uganda, Nigeria, and Guatemala. He was surprised to see that:

> Patients were doing better than they should have been. Patients with terrible multidrug-resistant TB or HIV were not as sick as the patients with comparable pathology in the U.S. by a big margin. They didn't have access to the medications that we had in the West but they weren't as sick as they should have been . . . so I started to ask what do these patients have that we don't have in the West, why aren't they as sick? I realized a lot of it was about really good community support, really good family support. Most of them still lived close to their families and friends. They don't have a lot of resources; they don't have a lot of stuff. But they have a lot of everyone involved in their care.

So, if you're reading this book, chances are, in contrast to the problems Dr. Spar saw in Nagorno Karabakh, yours are literally first-world problems. That's not to say they're not legitimate or important or challenging. It is to say that, in the broader sense of the phrase, you, too, could benefit from having a lot of everyone involved in your care and they could benefit from your involvement in theirs. As you develop your mindfulness alternative and complete your Life GPS, consider the communities that you connect to the most and what sorts of outcomes you would like to help create in them.

If you don't know where to start, spend some time reflecting on people and issues for which you have an affinity and how you can bring your gifts and talents to bear for the common good. For instance, when Elaine Hall saw the difference that the arts made to the level of engagement that Neal, her son with autism, had with the world, she decided to share that experience with other families affected by autism. Soon, she had a bunch of kids with autism onstage performing a musical and loving it. That experience grew into a nonprofit called the Miracle Project and an Emmy-winning film called *Autism: The Musical* that ran on HBO, was introduced by Elaine and Neal at the United Nations, and has helped and inspired families around the world.

Troubled by the indignity that the poor endure when they have to stand in line for food at a distribution center, Ron Shaich and his team at Panera Bread have started a chain of donation-based restaurants called Panera Cares. If you have the means, you make a donation; if you don't, you eat for free in a nice environment just like any other customer. Panera Care supports its own profit and loss statement and serves more than one million customers a year.

Born in Bridgetown, Barbados, Kaye Foster Cheek came to the United States and created a vibrant career for herself and life for her family. Based on her own experiences, she views part of her mission in life as "giving voice to the voiceless." She puts that into action in multiple ways. One way is through a homeless ministry at her church because she believes that "feeding the homeless is a way of enabling them to access their voice." She also does a lot of work with young women and girls that are suffering from neglect; she is "training them to be agents of social change, so that in finding their own voice they can also help others."

If you visit the website of author and consultant Peter Block and look at his biography, you'll see that the first line says, "Peter Block is an author, consultant and citizen of Cincinnati, Ohio." For Block, Cincinnati is not mentioned in a throwaway line that comes at the end of the bio as in "he resides with his family in Cincinnati, Ohio." No, he's a citizen of Cincinnati and that leads. He's done a lot in his community, including starting an urban arts center for at-risk youth and, as he told me, supporting agencies and efforts "in the city that align with the principles of focusing on gifts and focusing on the future."

Block raises three points—citizenship, gifts, and the future—that I think are important ideas to keep in mind as you consider what you're in it for and the outcomes you hope are facilitated by your showing up at your mindful best. We're all citizens of somewhere and not just one somewhere but multiple somewheres. We all have gifts but none of us have all the gifts. It can be an inspiring exercise to consider how your gifts align with the gifts of others in creating positive outcomes at home, at work, and in the community. And although we can't control the future, focusing on the mindfulness alternative can raise the awareness and intention that can improve the odds.

Coach's Corner

- What are the intangible, nonvisible outcomes at home that are most important to you?

- What does true success in the arena of work look like for you?

- What does community mean to you? How do you want to support and participate in your community?

---

14 Continuing with Your Mindfulness Alternative

Some Lessons Learned for Your Journey

Good Thing, Bad Thing, Who Knows?

One of the oft-repeated phrases in our house is "Good thing, bad thing, who knows?" I first came across the question in a Sufi story that Srikumar Rao related in his book *Are You Ready to Succeed?* I've since seen the story elsewhere and attributed to other traditions, but it always makes the same essential point in the same way. It goes like this:

What You'll Learn in This Chapter

- A different perspective on assessing what happens in your life

- Lessons learned that can help you as you continue with your mindfulness alternative

- Ideas, suggestions, and encouragement for taking your next steps

---

A farmer had a beautiful, powerful horse that was the envy of his neighbors in the community. One day the horse jumped the fence and ran away. The farmer's neighbors were quick to come over and offer their regrets over the farmer's loss of such a horse. He simply shrugged and said, "Good thing, bad thing, who knows?"

Then one day the horse came back to the farm along with five magnificent wild horses. The farmer and his son corralled the horses to train them for work on the farm. When they saw the horses, the neighbors rushed over to admire the horses and marvel at the farmer's good fortune. In response to their comments, he just shrugged and said, "Good thing, bad thing, who knows?"

A few days later, the farmer's son was training one of the new horses and fell off and severely broke his leg. After several months, it became clear that the son would never walk normally again. The neighbors came by to offer their condolences over the son's infirmity. The farmer shrugged and said, "Good thing, bad thing, who knows?"

Then war came to the kingdom and all of the young, able-bodied males were conscripted for the king's army, likely to never return home again. Because of his broken leg, the farmer's son was left at home. The neighbors, with much grief at their own losses, came by to comment on the farmer's good fortune in keeping his son. The farmer simply replied, "Good thing, bad thing, who knows?"

Of course, the point of the story is you never know how things are going to play out over the long run, so why spend a lot of energy on mulling over whether any particular outcome is good or bad? Things can and will change. I think the reason Diane and I use "Good thing, bad thing, who knows?" as a catch phrase is that our experience with my multiple sclerosis has taught us to suspend judgment on what could happen or is likely to happen in life. It's taught us both to be more mindful—aware and intentional—about how we live our lives. In this final chapter of the book, I want to share some of those mindfulness lessons I've learned from MS in the hope that they'll be useful to you on your journey.

Learning from My Built-In Feedback Loop

As I described in the Introduction, my diagnosis of MS came as a huge shock, and that first year after the diagnosis was scary and often hellish for Diane, me, and the rest of our family. The physical, mental, relational, and spiritual impacts of the disease were significant—not only on me, but also on the people I love. If you had asked me in that first year if my MS was a good thing or a bad thing, I would have definitely said, "Bad thing." If you asked me that question today, my answer would be "Who knows?" I don't mean to minimize the impact of MS or any other chronic disease or acute illness. There are millions of people who suffer with them in ways far worse than any I have experienced.

But when I look back on the five years since I was diagnosed, I see that I've done things in spite of MS and learned things because of it that I would never have imagined in those early days when I could barely walk, get off the couch, or think clearly enough to write a 500-word blog post. Since I was diagnosed, I've celebrated my twenty-fifth wedding anniversary with Diane with a kiss in front of the Eiffel Tower at midnight. I've seen our oldest son, Andy, graduate from college, move to San Francisco, and establish a vibrant life and career for himself there. I've been there through the difficult days of our youngest son Brad's own struggle with chronic illness and have cheered him on as he's graduated from high school, recovered, gained strength, and begun college. I've spent the night on an aircraft carrier and was launched from its deck in a shore-bound plane as a result of work I did with the U.S. Navy. I've gotten to speak to and work with thousands of executives and managers around the world. I've taken well over a thousand hours of yoga classes, and although I was the oldest person and only male (!) in the program, I completed the training required to

become a Registered Yoga Teacher. I've had innumerable sweet
moments with my parents, my brother and his wife, lifelong friends,
and new friends I've made in the past five years. I've taken part in a
dream that Diane has had since she was eight years old and moved
with her to Southern California. I've been able to write this book.

So, really, who knew? Although I had always tried to be aware and
intentional for most of my adult life and tried to follow routines that
would enhance that, MS compelled me to go deeper on that front in so
many ways. It was the catalyst for my own mindfulness alternative.
If you're going to stay functional with MS, you have to take care of
yourself not just physically, but mentally, relationally, and spiritually as
well. The worst thing you can do is live in a state of chronic fight or
flight. You have to learn to activate and access the rest and digest
response. For me that started with yoga classes three or four days a
week. That quickly went to six or seven days a week. I started paying
more attention to the kinds of food that made me feel better and those
that made me feel worse. Then I started paying more attention to my
breathing, not just in yoga class, but throughout the day. The yoga
classes and the breathing calmed me down and opened me up to a
deeper approach to relationships with friends, family, and clients.
Eventually, I became very consistent with daily time for reflection and
meditation and that routine has made everything else even sweeter.

So, is MS a good thing? I never would have imagined saying this in
2009, but in some ways, it has been for me. Having MS is like having a
built-in feedback loop that reminds me to be mindful. If I short change
my sleep, I feel it the next day in the form of a right knee that's stiffer
than usual. If I spend too much time at my desk without a break to get
up and stretch or go for a quick walk, I'm definitely going to feel it in
my lower back. If I eat a bunch of stuff that inflames my autoimmune
system, it makes me feel sluggish and out of rhythm for several days.
If I skip my morning reflection and quiet time for too many days in a
row, I tend to get spun-up and think less clearly. The fact that I have to

be aware and intentional about my daily routines and behaviors to feel good has had a positive effect on the rest of my life. Knowing that the MS could flare at any time and take me out in various ways has the effect of making me super mindful and appreciative of the good days I have and all of the opportunities they present.

So all of that is interesting for me at least, but what about you? I don't think you need to have a chronic illness to be more mindful, but what if you lived as if you did? As we discussed earlier in the book, there's more and more scientific evidence to suggest that the routines of mindfulness can help keep you from getting sick in the first place or help you greatly improve your overall well-being if you already have a health issue. Being more aware of what's going on in your body and intentional about your responses to what you observe can make all the difference in overcoming the overworked and overwhelmed state that will keep you on the gerbil wheel until you collapse. That is what will happen if you don't move to the mindfulness alternative—you'll collapse either physically, mentally, relationally, spiritually, or some combination of the four. Besides, none of us have any guarantees anyway. You or I could get hit by the proverbial or literal bus tomorrow. Do you really want to go out, whenever it comes, in that overworked and overwhelmed state? Me neither.

In the belief that we can all learn from one anothers' experiences, let me share some of the other lessons I've learned from MS that have helped me in my own journey with the mindfulness alternative and that may help you in yours.

What I've Learned about Mindfulness from MS That Could Help You

Suspend Judgment

When you have MS, you have a lot of weird moments. For instance, a couple of years ago I used to get this electric shooting pain out of nowhere in the back of my knee that would make me yelp out loud and practically drop me to the floor. When that first started happening, I immediately thought, "Oh crap, this is awful. What if this happens in the middle of a speech? What if this continues forever?" Well, as I write this, it's been two or three years since that's happened. Of course, it could happen again in the next five minutes. Who knows? That's exactly the point—who knows? MS has taught me to suspend judgment, to not jump to conclusions or immediately label a condition or a situation as good or bad. It just is. That's pretty much true for everything in life. Once you're aware of what is, then you can set some intentions about what, if anything, you want to, or can, do about it.

Nothing Is Permanent

There's been a joke making the rounds about a spiritual seeker who climbs the mountain to seek the wisdom of the guru who sits and meditates at the summit all day. The seeker reaches the top of the mountain and says to the guru, "Master, I've been pursuing my spiritual practice for years and, in spite of my best efforts, cannot quiet my mind. What should I do?" The guru answers, "This too shall pass," and returns to his meditation. Encouraged by what the guru said, the seeker returned to his practice and experienced enormous breakthroughs. Months later, he returned to the mountain to tell the guru about his progress. Upon reaching the summit, he exulted, "Master, I have reached new heights with my practice and believe I've attained enlightenment." The guru slowly opened his eyes, looked at the seeker, and said, "This too shall pass."

That's pretty much been my experience with MS. I have had physical highs and lows, sometimes in the same day or even in the same hour. You never quite know what you're going to get but one thing for sure is that whatever you get—good thing, bad thing, who knows?—it isn't going to last. It's kind of like the weather. If you're not happy with it now, wait. It will change. When you're in the trough of an overworked and overwhelmed state, it can feel like it's going to last forever. It, too, will pass. You can help it along with the mindfulness alternative. Other than death, no condition is permanent (and even death is up for some debate).

Each Day Is Its Own Day, Each Moment Is Its Own Moment

One of the things yoga instructors like to say is that no two days on the mat are the same. After taking over a thousand yoga classes in the past four years, I can attest to the truth of that statement. MS has made me more aware of how that applies to the rest of life as well. Noticing that has taught me to be less self-critical, to be more patient, and to pay attention to what's working on any given day—or, for that matter, in any given moment. From my own experience as an executive and watching and coaching other executives, I believe those are three characteristics worth cultivating. You can cultivate them by recognizing that every day is its own day and each moment is its own moment. The last one is over. The next one hasn't happened yet. Focus on this day. Focus on this moment.

Actions Have Consequences

You've probably seen the T-shirt that says, "Karma is a bitch." Yeah, it can be, but it doesn't have to be. Nothing has taught me that like having MS has. If I take care of myself and am aware of and intentional about what I'm doing, I usually feel good. If I don't, I definitely won't. It's sort of like the old line about looking before you leap. The lessons learned through experience with my condition have taught me to look ahead, consider the consequences, and reverse-engineer back from that picture to choose what to do now. Do I want to do yoga almost every day? No, there are days when I'd rather skip it, but I've learned that I feel crappy when I do. I'd much rather put in the time and feel good than not put it in and feel bad. How does that apply to you if you don't have a chronic disease that serves as a built-in feedback loop? The same way it applies to me in matters unrelated to how I feel physically. Pay attention to what makes you feel good or bad in the physical, mental, relational, and spiritual domains and adjust your future actions accordingly.

The Reps Matter

Earlier in the book, I told the story about Jeanne, my first yoga teacher who told me that if I came to class three days a week yoga would change my body, and if I came more than three days a week it would change my life. When you're doing things that are good for you, the reps matter. Of course, they also matter when you're consistently doing things that are bad for you. Repetitive behavior—whether it's helpful or harmful—shapes your body, your mind, your relationships, and your habits. Keep that in mind as you choose and pursue the routines that will help you show up at your best.

Instruction Matters

Even if you choose the right reps, it's important to have solid instruction. There are two big reasons for that. First, with no instruction or poor instruction, all those reps can groove in as bad habits that you'll have to work very hard to get rid of. Second, with good instruction, you'll learn how to go beyond what you thought you could do. That's absolutely been the case for me on my concurrent journey as an MS patient and as a yogi. It absolutely astounds me that the same guy who could barely walk a few years ago now does a few handstands or headstands most every day. Trust me, that's not a brag. The only reason I can do yoga party tricks like that is I've had some great instructors who have taught me how to do them and do them safely.

When it comes to further instruction for you, let me be the first to acknowledge that if you're interested in going deeper with mindfulness, this book just scratches the surface. If going further on this journey is your goal (and I hope it is), I strongly encourage you to:

- Read broadly
- Go to conferences
- Find a favorite yoga studio or some other community of practice (and/or use some of the great resources that are available online)
- Take a course in Mindfulness-Based Stress Reduction
- Join a meditation group
- Use guided meditations that you can find online
- Go on a guided retreat

The options are basically limitless. If I was going to recommend just one thing as a next step after this book, I would suggest getting a copy (physical, not electronic) of Jon Kabat-Zinn's classic book *Wherever You Go, There You Are.* It is beautifully written and easy to read, from a master teacher in the field. Each chapter is a short two- to four-page essay or reflection that you can read in 5 to 10 minutes. *Wherever You Go* has been my morning reading book numerous times over the years and was my first true introduction to mindfulness many years ago. If you appreciate where I'm coming from in this book, you will love *Wherever You Go, There You Are.*

Improvement Comes Incrementally, Then Suddenly

Those handstands and headstands I mentioned in the last segment are not poses I just perfectly popped into the first time I tried. It took six months of practice for me to get comfortable doing a pose called tripod headstand away from the wall. When I finally did move from the wall, I would do it in class only if I was in the front row and had plenty of room to roll forward out of it if (and usually when) I lost my balance. I had some wipeouts that would make a NASCAR driver proud. Today, three years later, I can go up into tripod headstand and stay there pretty much on command and have been goaded into doing one in meeting rooms a few times by participants in my leadership workshops. It looks easy now, but it took two or three years to make it look easy. It's like the band that becomes an overnight success except that they've been playing to rooms of 10 or 20 people for 10 years before they hit it big. The improvement that came incrementally over the years is what laid the groundwork for seemingly sudden success.

You will find the same thing as you continue with your mindfulness alternative. There will be days when you feel like you're making no progress at all and other days where you feel like you're regressing, not progressing. On those days, take heart. It's normal and part of the process. Even if you can barely see it or can't see at all, you're making progress. If you give up too soon, you forgo the opportunity for "sudden" breakthroughs. Stick with it.

Your Current Capabilities Do Not Determine Your Future Limitations

In my less mindful moments with MS (yes, I have them), I find that I can pretty quickly get sucked into the what-if cycle. You know how it goes. "What if this happens? Then, what if that happens? Wow, what if that happens, too? That would really stink." Before I know it, I've wasted a good bit of time on those questions and usually feel worse than when I started asking them.

There are days when I show up for yoga class where I feel so wonky that I'm nervous about being there. Some days before class starts, I just lay on the mat doing the full-body scan trying to predict how things are going to go for the next 90 minutes. Spoiler alert: It almost always goes great. The sweat flows in a good way. The joints move nicely. The muscles stretch. The rest and digest response kicks in and gets me out of that low-grade version of fight or flight.

On the way home from class, I often start thinking about and feeling grateful for all of the things my body can do. Then I start wondering why I spent so much time worrying about what it might not be able to do in the future. The fact of the matter is there are things I can't do today that I used to be able to do (running a marathon, for example). But there are still a hell of a lot of things I can do right now and I'm actually learning new ones all the time.

So here's what I've concluded. My current capabilities don't determine my future limitations unless, of course, I spend so much time worrying about what my limitations might be in the future that I don't maximize my capabilities today. Other than a chronically stiff right knee and a wonky tweak now and then, I'm in better physical shape today than I was when I was diagnosed with MS five years ago. I feel like I'm in better mental, relational, and spiritual shape as well. Again, who knew?

If it's true for me, it's true for you too. Your current capabilities and condition do not determine your future limitations. Have faith and keep going.

Follow Your Life GPS

As we come to the end of this book, my last lesson learned is to work through and follow your Life GPS® year over year and year in and year out. After almost two decades of spending time with my wife, Diane, to work through mine each year and to do my best to stay accountable to it, I can say it's made a difference. Both of us have all of our Life GPS worksheets from all of the years since we've started and they've become a record of how we and our lives have changed over that time. The changes aren't usually dramatic year to year. The take on how I am at my best usually doesn't change radically within 12 months but it's changed a lot from 5 years ago or 10 years ago. Likewise, the routines that help me show up at my best have changed as my body and perspective have changed. In my case, because of the way I've chosen to manage my MS, my routines in all four domains—physical, mental, relational, and spiritual—have changed significantly in the past three or four years. It's been interesting for me to observe how those routines have also shifted the way I view myself at my best and what I consider to be the most important in the outcomes I hope for at home, work, and in the community.

In a nutshell, I think the change has been that I've become more mindful, particularly if you accept the definition of mindfulness that I've been using in this book—that mindfulness equals awareness and intention. I can't remember a time in my life when I've been more aware of what's going on around me and what's going on inside of me and intentional about where I need to be spending my time and attention. The really exciting thing for me is I have a strong sense, because of the routines I'm working on in my Life GPS, that that awareness and intention is going to continue to grow and deepen. When I look through my past journal entries, I can see that's the trend.

I write and share all of this not as a declaration of victory but as the experience of someone who has spent a lot of his life feeling overworked and overwhelmed. Do I have moments when I still do? Yes, absolutely. The difference now is I recognize it as a feeling that I can do something about. It's usually as simple as tapping into one of my Life GPS routines like breathing deeply or going to a yoga class and shifting out of fight or flight and into rest and digest. And that's what sets me up to be more mindful, aware, and intentional.

As we close, I'll share one last story about what it feels like to make the shift from overworked and overwhelmed to the mindfulness alternative. One recent evening Diane and I were out for a walk in a park close to where we live. We stopped to admire a beautiful view and, as we did, turned to each other for a hug. In more than 27 years of marriage, it's impossible to count the number of times we've hugged. The hug in the park that night was the hug to end all hugs. As we stood there, every thought I had about everything else melted away. The only thing I was thinking about was how much I love Diane and how grateful I was at that moment to express the love I have for her and receive her expression of the love she has for me. We were both so present for each other—fully present, aware of this great gift we've been given, and fully intentional about expressing our gratitude for that. It was a moment when time seemed to slow down and what was probably only a few minutes felt like hours.

And, if I had been going through my to-do list in my mind, checking in on my phone, or just generally lost in my overworked and overwhelmed thoughts during that walk, none of that would have happened. As we end our time together in this book, my hope for you is that you become more and more open to, aware of, and intentional about tuning in to the little moments in life that are so sweet but so ephemeral that you'll miss them if you aren't paying attention. Sure, there will continue to be moments, days, weeks, or even months when you feel overworked and overwhelmed. But even in the midst of those times, there are moments of sweetness and light that are there for the taking if you notice them. They can be moments at home, at work, or in the community because there are human beings with whom you have a connection in all of those places. If for no other reason than making those connections, I intend to stick with the mindfulness alternative. I hope you will as well and hope that this book and the resources associated with it have helped you define and take new steps toward your own mindfulness alternative. I wish you well on your journey and look forward to hearing reports of your progress. Better yet, perhaps we'll see each other along the way.

Appendix
Coach's Corner
Compendium

Chapter 1 Reality Bites (or Does It?)

- What's making you feel overworked and overwhelmed?

- What's the payoff for you from overcommitting to many of the things that make you feel overworked and overwhelmed?

- What are the big wedges in your pie chart of how you spend the 168 hours you get each week? What would you like to change about that?

- What are the biggest drivers of distraction that keep you from being fully present?

Chapter 2 What Does *Mindfulness* Even Mean Anyway?

- What does *mindfulness* mean to you?

- What types of extrinsic interference typically create the intrinsic interference (mental chatter) that keeps you from performing at your best?

- What story do you have about why you're overworked and overwhelmed? Is that a micro story about what's happening lately or a macro story about why you're in this situation in general?

- What other stories could also be true?

Chapter 3   What's Going on in There, and What Can You Do About It?

- What signs, if any, tell you that you might be in a state of chronic fight or flight?
- What are the situations or factors that cause you to go into fight or flight when you're not actually under physical threat?
- What's one easy thing you could do now to activate your rest and digest response? (*Hint:* It involves three deep breaths.) What else could you do?

Chapter 4   Where Do You Want to Go?

- What routines do you have in your life today that help you show up at your best?
- What routines have you had in the past that might help you show up at your best today?
- What difference would consistently showing up at your best make to the outcomes you hope for at home, at work, and in your community?

Chapter 5   How Are You at Your Best?

- What does it mean to you to be in the zone or in flow?
- When was the last time you felt that way?
- What were the conditions that made it feel that way?
- What characteristics describe you when you're at your best?

Chapter 6 What's Their Secret?

- What will it take for you to make a commitment to manage your time so you show up at your best?

- Whose help and support do you need? What request do you need to make of them?

- Which of the 10 time management tips is most in the sweet spot between easy for you to implement and likely to make a difference?

- What other time management hacks do you need to implement?

Chapter 7 You Are What You Repeatedly Do

- Which of the seven principles for choosing and following the routines that work for you resonates the most? Why does it?

- Which of the seven principles will be most challenging for you to follow? Why will it?

- Who are the people in your life who have regular lines of sight into how you show up and who you'd like to invite to help you follow through on your routines?

Chapter 8 It Starts with the Body

- What's the one routine in the physical domain that you're not doing now that you think would make the biggest difference to your showing up at your best?

- What kind of support or information do you need to get started? Who could help you with that?

- What might get in the way of following through on that routine and how could you work around that?

Chapter 9   A Beautiful Mind

- What's your take? Do you usually breathe from your chest or your belly?

- What kind of cues could remind you to breathe when the fight or flight response clutters your mind?

- Which time frame of mind—past, present or future—presents your biggest opportunity for more mindfulness?

Chapter 10   In Right Relationship

- What style of listening—transient, transactional, or transformational—do you practice most often? What's the impact of that?

- What's one routine in the relational domain that you're not doing now that you think would make the biggest difference to you showing up at your best?

- What person or group—yourself, partner, kids, family, friends, colleagues—could use more of your time and attention? What would that look like in the coming month?

Chapter 11   What's Your Purpose Here, Anyway?

- What's the purpose in your life that informs what you're trying to do at home, at work, and in your community?

- What routines do you currently have to create space for reflecting on your purpose and how you're showing up against that purpose?

- What could you do to take your routine of reflection to the next level?

Chapter 12 Making It Work

- What's working for you and not working for you with your operating rhythm? What do you want to keep doing or do differently?
- What are the big rocks in your life that you definitely need to schedule first?
- Who's a buddy that you'd like to invite to be your peer coaching partner in following through on your routines?

Chapter 13 What Are You in It For?

- What are the intangible, nonvisible outcomes at home that are most important to you?
- What does true success in the arena of work look like for you?
- What does community mean to you? How do you want to support and participate in your community?

Notes

Introduction: Overworked and Overwhelmed? Welcome to the Mindfulness Alternative

1. Kabat-Zinn, Jon, presentation delivered at 2013 Wisdom 2.0 Conference, San Francisco, California.

Chapter 1: Reality Bites (or Does It?)

1. DeGusta, Michael, "Are smart phones spreading faster than any technology in human history?" *M.I.T. Technology Review* (May 9, 2012).

2. Deal, Jennifer J., "Always on, never done? Don't blame the smartphone," Center for Creative Leadership white paper (August 2013).

3. 2013 Stress Study, American Psychological Association. Washington, D.C.

4. Benson-Henry Institute for Mind Body Medicine http://www .bensonhenryinstitute.org. Accessed March 20, 2014.

5. *Smart brief on leadership*, Reader Poll, 2012. "How often do you overcommit yourself and your team?" January 3, 2012.

6. University of California, Irvine, "E-mail 'vacations' decrease stress, increase concentration," news release, http://today.uci.edu/news/2012/05/ nr_email_120503.php. Accessed March 20, 2014.

7. "96 Minutes of Daily Interruptions," *IIBR Daily Stat* (July 19, 2011).

Chapter 2: What Does *Mindfulness* Even Mean Anyway?

1. Kabat-Zinn, Jon, comments as member of panel discussion on "Becoming Conscious: the science of mindfulness," Nour Foundation, February 23,

https://www.youtube.com/watch?v=wPNEmxWSNxg. Accessed March 20, 2014.

2. Frankl, Viktor, *Man's search for meaning* (Boston: Beacon Press, 2006).

3. Ibid.

4. Heifetz, Ronald A., and Donald L. Laurie, "The work of leadership," *Harvard Business Review* (January 1997).

5. Gallwey, W. Timothy, *The inner game of work* (New York: Random House, 2001).

6. Sullivan, Bob, and Hugh Thompson, "Brain interrupted," *New York Times* (May 3, Sunday Review section).

7. Richtel, Matt, "You can't take it with you, but you still want more," *New York Times* (January 4, Business section).

8. Kasser, Tim, and Richard M. Ryan, "A dark side of the American dream: correlates of financial success as a central life aspiration," *Journal of Personality and Social Psychology* 65, no. 2 (1993): 410–422.

9. Huffington, Arianna, *Thrive: the third metric to redefining success and creating a life of well-being, wisdom, and wonder* (New York: Harmony, 2014).

Chapter 3: What's Going on in There, and What Can You Do About It?

1. Hanson, Rick, *Buddha's brain: the practical neuroscience of happiness, love, and wisdom* (Oakland: New Harbinger Publications, 2009).

2. Davis, Susan, "Addicted to your smartphone? Here's what to do," WebMD feature, http://www.webmd.com/balance/guide/addicted-your-smartphone-what-to-do. Accessed May 11, 2014.

3. Soares, J. M., et. al., "Stress-induced changes in human decision-making are reversible," *Translational Psychiatry* (July 3, 2013).

4. Benson-Henry Institute for Mind Body Medicine, http://www.bensonhenryinstitute.org. Accessed March 20, 2014.

5. Haar, Dan, "Aetna's Bertolini, actress bring mindfulness to mainstream," *Hartford Courant* (January 22, 2014).

6. Goodman, Leah McGrath, "The killer stalking Wall Street," *Newsweek* (November 22, 2013).

7. Benson, Herbert, *The relaxation response* (New York: Harper Torch, 2000).

8. "Evidence builds that meditation strengthens the brain," *Science Daily,* http://www.sciencedaily.com/releases/2012/03/120314170647.htm, March 14, 2012.

9. Epel, Elisa, et al., "Can meditation slow rate of cellular aging? Cognitive stress, mindfulness and telomeres," *Annals of the New York Academy of Sciences* (August 28, 2009).

10. Lavretsky, Eleanor, et al., "A pilot study of yogic meditation for family dementia caregivers with depressive symptoms: effects on mental health, cognition, and telomerase activity," *International Journal of Geriatric Psychiatry* (January 28, 2013).

11. Chen, Pauline W., "Easing doctor burnout with mindfulness," *New York Times* (September 26, 2013, Well section).

Chapter 5: How Are You at Your Best?

1. Csikszentmihalyi, Mihaly, *Flow: the psychology of optimal experience* (New York: Harper Perennial Modern Classics, 2001).

2. Hanson, Rick, "Confronting the negativity bias," *Psychology Today* (October 26, 2010).

3. Carlson, Richard, and Joseph Bailey, *Slowing down to the speed of life* (New York: HarperOne, 2009).

Chapter 6: What's Their Secret?

1. Kirkland, Rik, "Leading in the 21st century: an interview with Ford's Alan Mulally," *McKinsey Quarterly* (November 2013).

2. Favaro, Ken, and Amy D'Onofrio, "The Thought Leader Interview: Loran Nordgren," *Strategy + Business* (Autumn 2013).

3. Carlson, Richard, and Joseph Bailey, *Slowing down to the speed of life* (New York: HarperOne, 2009).

Chapter 7: You Are What You Repeatedly Do

1. Duhigg, Charles, *The power of habit: why we do what we do in life and business* (New York: Random House, 2012).

Chapter 8: It Starts with the Body

1. Bergland, Christopher, "Let's not get panicky," *Psychology Today* (January 9, 2012).

2. Weber, Lauren, "Walk this way: treadmill desks may improve job performance," *Wall Street Journal* (March 4, 2014).

3. Domonell, Kristin, "Five surprising health benefits of yoga," *Daily Burn* December 16, http://dailyburn.com/life/fitness/health-benefits-yoga/. Accessed April 5, 2014.

4. *Harvard women's health watch,* The Health Benefits of Tai Chi (May 2009).

5. Harmon, Katherine, "Rare genetic mutation lets some people function with less sleep," *Scientific American* (August 13, 2009).

6. Jones, Jeffrey, "In U.S., 40% get less than recommended amount of sleep," Gallup Well Being, December 19, 2013, http://www.gallup.com/poll/166553/less-recommended-amount-sleep.aspx. Accessed April 5, 2014.

7. "Sleep, performance, and public safety," Harvard Medical School, Division of Sleep Medicine, December 18, 2007, http://healthysleep.med.harvard.edu/healthy/matters/consequences/sleep-performance-and-public-safety. Accessed April 5, 2014.

8. Peri, Camille, "10 things to hate about sleep loss," WebMD Feature, http://www.webmd.com/sleep-disorders/excessive-sleepiness-10/10-results-sleep-loss. Accessed April 5, 2014.

9. Mayo Clinic Staff, "Sleep tips: 7 steps to better sleep," June 9, 2014, http://www.mayoclinic.org/healthy-living/adult-health/in-depth/sleep/art-20048379 Accessed June 29, 2014.

10. Lovato, Nicole, et al., "The effects of napping on cognitive functioning," *Progressive Brain Research* 185 (2010): 155–166.

Chapter 9: A Beautiful Mind

1. University of Southern California Laboratory of Neuroimaging, http://www.loni.usc.edu/about_loni/education/brain_trivia.php. Accessed March 8, 2014.

2. Sharma, Vivek Kumar, et al., "Effect of fast and slow pranayama practice on cognitive functions in healthy volunteers," *Journal of Clinical Diagnostic Research* 8, no. 1 (2014): 10–13.

3. "Brief meditative exercise helps cognition," *Science Daily* (April 19, 2010).

4. "Mindfulness meditation may improve decision-making, new study suggests," *Science Daily* (February 12, 2014).

Chapter 10: In Right Relationship

1. Gibbs, Nancy, "Your life is fully mobile," *Time* (August 16, 2012). Kane, Suzanne, "Smartphone addiction: will U.S. go the way of South Korea?" *Addiction Treatment Magazine* (August 5, 2013).

2. Holt-Lunstad, Julianne, Timothy B. Smith, and J. Bradley Layton, "Social relationships and mortality risk: a meta-analytic review," *PLOS Medicine* (July 27, 2010).

3. Greenleaf, Robert K., *Servant leadership: a journey into the nature of legitimate power and greatness* (Mahwah, NJ: Paulist Press, 2002).

4. Rath, Tom, "Vital friends: the people you can't afford to live without," *Gallup Business Journal* (2006), http://businessjournal.gallup.com/content/24754/vital-friends-book-center.aspx. Accessed May 10, 2014.

Chapter 11: What's Your Purpose Here, Anyway?

1. Chu, Jeff, "Can Apple's Angela Ahrendts spark a retail revolution?" *Fast Company* (January 6, 2014).

2. Baike, Karen A., and Kay Wilhelm, "Emotional and physical health benefits of expressive writing," *Advances in Psychiatric Treatment* 11, 338–346.

Chapter 13: What Are You in It For?

1. Gandhi, Mohandas K., "Bhagavad–Gita introduction," http://www.teosofia.com/gita/gita-intro-gandhi.html. Accessed May 1, 2014.

2. BowlingAlone.com, http://bowlingalone.com. Accessed, May 15, 2014.

Acknowledgments

While most books bear the name of one or more authors, no book makes it into the reader's hands without the support and dedication of a lot of other people. That's certainly the case with *Overworked and Overwhelmed: The Mindfulness Alternative.* It's a pleasure and an honor to acknowledge the many people who have helped me bring this book to you.

First, thank you to all of the people who have taught me about mindfulness over the years. Some of you I know very well, and others I've learned from at a distance. It's all made a difference. A special shout out and Namaste goes to all of the amazing yoga teachers I've had over the years. Thank you for everything you've given me and taught me.

A sincere thanks to all of the people I interviewed for the book. It was a privilege to hear your stories and enlightening to get your perspectives on mindfulness. There are too many of you to list by name, but all of your insights were invaluable. Thanks also to the many friends and colleagues who suggested people that I should interview and who, in many cases, made introductions that enabled me to connect with those people. To both groups, there would be no book without you. Thank you.

Many thanks to Richard Narramorc, my cditor at John Wiley & Sons, who sought me out years ago to ask if I was interested in writing another book and who patiently hung in there with me while I moved from not now, to maybe, to let's go. Thanks also to Richard's colleagues: Tiffany Colon, who made sure that all the pieces came together; Lauren Freestone for overseeing additional editing and production; and Peter Knox and Melissa Connors, for their enthusiasm and partnership in getting the word out. And thanks also to Karen Kraimer, who did a great job of transcribing hours of interviews so I could use them to prepare the manuscript.

Thanks to all of the members of our amazing creative team who have been thought partners in shaping the look and feel of the book and all the things that need to be done to present the book to the world. I feel very fortunate to work and be friends with people like Mark Fortier, Pamela Peterson, Melissa Wilhelm, Marc Sacro, Dixie Toledo, Remel Gumabon, Melissa Hoyle, Eva van Geneen, and Andy Eblin (who created the Life GPS® icons in the book and also happens to be my son).

A special thank you to my friend Rae Ringel, who spent an evening with me brainstorming the title to get to the one that's on the cover of the book you're reading. Thanks also to all of my friends and colleagues in the Georgetown University leadership coaching community who were very kind to give me feedback on this content during the writing process. And a very deep thanks to my friends and colleagues who took time to read and comment on the manuscript: Marilyn Gorman, Shawn Hunter, Jennifer Tucker, Per Wingerup, and Lori Zukin.

One of the most challenging things about writing a book is doing it while still serving clients and running a business. Fortunately, we have a great team at the Eblin Group who help make that possible. Thank you to Deb Greenleaf, Joanne Lehmkuhl, Mary Motz, and Michele Wilcox for keeping the trains running on time and our clients happy.

As always, I feel very blessed to have family and friends who cheer me on and take an interest in what I do. Special thanks on that front to Andy Eblin and Brad Eblin for loving me, laughing with me, and growing with me. You guys are awesome. I love you.

Finally, there's my wife, Diane Eblin. She is the most talented, fun, energetic, loving, totally-has-your-back, mindful, beautiful person I know. You know all of those paragraphs you just read about the people who have taught me about mindfulness, helped with interviews for the book, were on the creative team, helped shape the content of the book, read the manuscript, or helped run the Eblin Group? Diane is a key player—the key player, really—in all of that. The only thing she hasn't done on this project is work at John Wiley & Sons, but she's spent a lot of time coordinating things with the folks there, too. Because this book would not exist without Diane, she should probably be listed as a coauthor. She is definitely the coauthor of my life. Diane, you are amazing. I love you and am so thankful to be your husband, partner, and friend.

About the Author

Scott Eblin is the cofounder and president of the Eblin Group, a professional development firm that supports executives and managers in exhibiting leadership presence by being fully present. As an executive coach, educator, and author, Eblin works with senior and rising leaders in some of the world's best known and regarded organizations.

He is the author of *The Next Level: What Insiders Know About Executive Success* (2010) and has also contributed chapters to *Developing Talent for Organizational Results: Training Tools from the Best in the Field* (2012) and *On Becoming a Leadership Coach: A Holistic Approach to Coaching Excellence* (2013).

Eblin is an honors graduate with a degree in international relations from Davidson College. He also holds a master's degree in public administration from Harvard University. He is a graduate of the leadership coaching certificate program at Georgetown University and is a member of the faculty of that program. He is a member of the International Coach Federation and holds the designation of Professional Certified Coach. Eblin is also a Registered Yoga Teacher through the Yoga Alliance.

He resides in the Los Angeles area with his wife, Diane.

Index

NOTE: Page references in *italics* refer to figures.

A

action
  consequences of, 229–230
  taking, 144
Aetna, 39
After Action Review (U.S. Army),
  143
Ahrendts, Angela, 183
Ajello, Andy, 121, 127
Allen, Thad
  mindfulness in work of, 15–18,
    21–22, 24
  on time management techniques,
    74–75, 80–84, 97–98
All Joy and No Fun (Senior), 163–164
Amabile, Teresa, 9, 171, 188, 199,
  217–218
American Psychological Association
  (APA), 10, 11
amygdala, 34
Aristotle, 53, 62, 105, 128
At Your Best Approach
  characteristics of, 68–70
  impact of, 66–68
  worksheet for, *64*
Autism: The Musical (HBO), 94,
  220
autonomic nervous system (ANS),
  33–34, *36*
awareness, mindfulness and, 18,
  21–22

B

back pain, 128
Bailey, Joseph, 74, 88
barriers, to mindfulness, 22–27
Becoming a Mindful Leader (workshop),
  67, 137
Benson, Herbert, 40, 117–118
Benson-Henry Institute for Mind Body
  Medicine, Massachusetts General
  Hospital, 10, 39
Berenstain Bears in Too Much Pressure,
  213
Bickel, Keith, 162–163
Bickel, Suzan, 162–163
"BlackBerry Orphans" *(Wall Street
  Journal)*, 164
Blackburn, Elizabeth, 41
Blanchard, Ken, 162
Block, Peter, 81, 181, 183, 221
Bolgiano, Elizabeth, 71, 167
boundaries, setting, 89–92
Brace, Carolyn, 166
brain
  diet and, 126
  fight or flight response and, 37–38,
    39
  mind-body operating system and,
    31–43, *35, 36, 39*
  negativity bias and, 73
  sleep and, 124, 125
breaks, scheduling, 96–97

breathing exercises
  benefits of, 41–42, 143
  breathing-based meditation for
    reflection, 184–185
  STOP technique, 134–135
  yoga, 136–137, 139–140
Bregman, Peter, 165
Brigham Young University, 154
Bryant, Anne, 121, 215–216
Buechner, Frederick, 177

C
Cain, Susan, 168
calendar, resetting, 82, 147
Campbell, Jim, 26–27, 86–87, 97,
  217
Carlson, Richard, 74, 88
Carroll, Pete, 201
cause and effect, law of, 107
celebration, of wins, 199–200
Center for Creative Leadership, 9
centering, through visual focal points,
  180–182
change
  establishing routines for, 129, 230
    (See also routines)
  following Life GPS® for, 233–235
  incremental steps for, 109, 189,
    195–196
"chatter," in the mind, 23–24
Cheek, Kaye Foster, 81, 178–179, 186,
  198, 221
children, connection with, 163–167
choice, intention and, 19–20
colleagues, connection with, 170–172
Columbus, Tracy, 24, 85, 160, 181
commitment
  to routines, 114
  to time management, 79
community arena
  Life GPS® and, 56
  mindful outcomes for, 218–222
  peak performance and, 64
"competitive parenting," 213–214

confidence, building, 119
connection
  with children, 164–167
  with colleagues, 170–172
  with family, 167
  with friends, 168–170
  with life partners, 162–163
  relational routines for, 161
  self talk and, 161–162
  See also relational routines
Cooper, Crystal, 84–85, 93, 105–106
corporate restructuring, as trend, 8
Covey, Stephen R., 49
Csikszentmihalyi, Mihaly, 62–63
cues, for routines, 111

D
Dass, Ram, 160
decision making, routines for, 105.
    See also mental routines; physical
    routines; relational routines;
    routines; spiritual routines
Dickerson, Deborah, 200–202
diet, establishing routines for,
  125–126
discernment, 175–177
discursive thinking, 23–24
doctor visits, stress and, 10–11
Duhigg, Charles, 110

E
eating, mindful, 126–127
Eblin, Andy, 67–68, 225
Eblin, Brad, 67–68, 225
Eblin, Diane, 49–50, 67–68, 126, 213,
  225, 234–235
Eblin, Scott
  health of, 41, 122, 224–225
  The Next Level: What Insiders Know
    About Executive Success, 6–7, 12
  yoga practice of, 122, 225–226
    (See also yoga)
  See also Life GPS®; individual names
    of family members

Eblin Group
    inception of, 50
    website of, 51
ego, problems of, 128
e-mail, stress and, 11, 48, 95
exercise
    establishing routines for, 117–123
    transformation through routine of,
        48, 54–55
    See also yoga
extrinsic interference
    distractions, examples, 8–11, 24, 48
    distractions and time management,
        95–96
    reaching peak performance and, 71–76

F
family
    connection with, 163–167, 167
    mindful outcomes and extended
        family, 214–215
Fast Company (Ahrendts), 183
feedback, 198, 225–227
fight or flight response
    as chronic, 36–37
    defined, 34, *35*
    effect on body by, 37–38, *39*
    health and, 117
    reaching peak performance and, 72
Finard, Jeri, 28–29, 138, 212–213
flow, 62–63
focal points, centering through, 180–182
focus. *See* mindfulness
Frankl, Viktor, 19–20
Franklin County (Pennsylvania) jail,
    59–61
Franklin Covey, 95–96
friends, connection with, 168–170
Frye, Helen, 170

G
Gallup, 123, 171
Gallwey, Tim, 21, 39

"garbage in, garbage out," 107
Gervais, Michael, 201
Gandhi, Mohandas, 210–211
Give and Take (Grant), 79–80, 93
goals. *See* outcomes
Grant, Adam, 71, 79–80, 93–94,
    168–169, 182–183
gratitude, 178–180
Greenleaf, Robert, 160

H
Hall, Elaine, 94, 165–167, 220
Halligan, Brian, 88–89, 125
Hanson, Rick, 36, 73
happiness, 56–57
Harrison, George, 128–129
Harvard Business Review, 165
HBO, 94, 220
health, relational routines for, 154
health problems, avoiding. *See* physical
    routines
Heifetz, Ron, 21
Hiltz, Paul, 138–139, 183
holidays, connecting with families
    during, 167
home arena
    Life GPS® and, 56
    mindful outcomes for, 211–215
    peak performance and, 64
HubSpot, 125
Huffington, Arianna, 27, 176
humanity, 154–155
Hurricane Katrina, 15–18, 21–22

I
inner monologue, 161–162,
    196–197
INSEAD, 143
instruction, importance of, 230–231
Integrated Life Blueprint, 51
intention
    mindfulness and, 19–20, 22
    mindful outcomes and, 209–211
    time management and, 77–79

interpersonal behavior, relational
routines for, 154. *See also* relational
routines; teams
intrinsic interference, 23–24

J
Jawaharlal Institute of Postgraduate
Medical Education & Research,
139
Jobs, Steve, 179–180
Johnson, Spencer, 162
Jory, Melissa McLean, 120–121, 167
journaling, 188–190
judgment, suspending, 227–228
Jung, Carl, 85

K
Kabat-Zinn, Jon, 18, 231
kaizen, 109
Kasser, Tim, 27
Kest, Bryan, 19, 39–40, 127, 212
"Killer Apps"
breathing exercises, 136–142
listening, 155–160
movement, 117–119
reflection, 177–192
Kramer, Steven, 9, 188, 199
Kristen, Birgitte, 137

L
Laboratory of Neuroimaging, University
of Southern California, 135
leadership
defined, 13
leadership presence, 12–13
relational routines for, 154
Lescault, Henry, 95, 185–186
Life GPS®, 47–57
best version of your self recognized
with, 51–53
change and, 233–235
explained, 49–51
outcomes of, 55–57
premise of, 211

self-knowledge and, 62
transformation through routines,
47–49, 53–55
weekly review of, 198–199
Worksheet, *52*, 66
life partners, connection with, 162–163
Luders, Eileen, 41

M
magnetic resonance imagine (MRI), 38,
41
Mailliard, Ward, 146, 176, 210
"managing the gravel," 95
Man's Search for Meaning (Frankl),
19–20
marriage, connection and, 162–163
Massachusetts General Hospital, 10, 39
Mayo Clinic, 124
McKinsey Quarterly, 87
meditation, as reflection, 184–187
medical complaints, stress and, 10–11
meditative breathing. *See* breathing
exercises
mental domain
Life GPS® and, 54
mental chatter, 23–24
mental routines, 131–149
benefits of, 148–149
breathing exercises, "Killer App,"
136–142
breathing exercises, STOP technique,
134–135
establishing, 112–113
need for, 131–134
time frames of mind, 135–136,
143–146
visualization to overcome worry,
146–148
mind-body operating system, 31–43
autonomic nervous system (ANS),
33–34, *36*
fight or flight, 34–38, *35, 39*, 72,
116–117
Life GPS® and, 56

psychosomatic illness and, 38–40
rest and digest function, 35–36, *36*,
    40–42
small improvements for, 42
stress reaction and, 31–33
mindfulness, 15–29
    about time management, 79–81
    awareness for, 18, 21–22
    barriers to, 22–27
    defined, 15–18
    exercise and, 118
    for high performance, 20–22
    intention and, 19–20, 22
    mind-body operating system and,
        31–43, *35, 36*, 39
    mindfulness meditation, 140–141,
        144–146, 148–149
    moments of truth and, 27–29
    need for, 3–13, *10*
    reaching peak performance and, 74–75
    See also outcomes
Mindfulness Based Stress Reduction
    (MBSR), 18
mindless accumulation, 27
Miracle Project, 94, 165–167
MIT Technology Review, 9
moderation, importance of, 128
"monkey mind," 23–24
Montaigne, 146
movement. *See* exercise
Mulally, Alan, 87

N
naps, 125
Nassetta, Chris, 83–84, 86, 91, 196
necessity of tasks, recognizing, 81
negativity bias, 73
New Orleans, Hurricane Katrina and,
    15 18, 21–22
*Next Level: What Insiders Know About
    Executive Success, The* (Eblin), 6–7,
    12
next-level situations
    defined, 6–8

*The Next Level: What Insiders Know
    About Executive Success* (Eblin),
    6–7, 12
Next Level 360 degree assessments, 8
Next Level Leadership®, 47–49
Nordgren, Loran, 88
"no," strategic use of, 92–94
Nour Foundation, 18

O
One Minute Manager, The (Blanchard,
    Johnson), 162
Open Heart Project, 23–24
operating rhythm
    following through on routines for,
        194–195
    work-life rhythm, 82–85, 107
organizational presence, 12–13
Oswald, Monica, 5, 121–122
outcomes
    actions and results of, 209–211
    in community, 218–222
    at home, 211–215
    importance of, 207–209
    Life GPS® and, 55–57
    as uncertain, 223–225
    at work, 215–218
outsourcing tasks, for time
    management, 85–87
overworking, 3–13
    leadership presence as solution, 12–13
    next-level situations of, 6–8
    stress of, 8–11
    work commitments and, 3–6, 9, *10*
    See also work arena

P
pacing, importance of, 96–98
Panera Bread, 173–175, 221
Panera Cares, 221
parasympathetic nervous system (PNS)
    defined, 33–34
    rest and digest function, 35–36, *36*,
        40–42

parenting
 "competitive parenting," 213–214
 connection and, 163–167
Paul (apostle), 198
peak performance, 59–76
 avoiding distractions and, 71–76
 characteristics for, 59–61, 68–70
 following through on routines for,
  194–195
 identifying, 63–66
 mind-body operating system and, 40
 mindfulness for, 20–22
 operating at your best for, 62–63
 self-knowledge and, 61–62
 At Your Best Approach impact, 66–68
Pendergrass, Lynn, 169
Pennebaker, James, 188
Perlow, Leslie, 37
permanence, concept of, 228–229
personal presence, 12–13
physical domain, Life GPS® and, 54
physical routines, 115–129
 avoiding health crisis with, 115–117
 for change, 128–129
 diet, 126
 ego and, 128
 establishing, 112–113
 moderation of, 128
 movement, 48, 54–55, 117–123
  (See also yoga)
 sleep, 123–125
Piver, Susan, 23–24, 212
postponing tasks, for time management,
  85–87
Power of Habit, The (Duhigg), 110
practice
 for incremental improvement,
  231–232
 perfectionism versus, 193–194, 201
prana, 72–73
pranayama, 139
praxis, 109–110
prayer, 184–187
prefrontal cortex, 123, 125
presence

focus and, 229
 playing with, 144–146
 undivided, 163–167
prioritizing
 establishing routines and, 196
 mental routines and, 147
 time management and, 85–87
productivity, exercise and, 118
Progress Principle, The (Amabile,
  Kramer), 9, 171, 188, 199
Psychology Today, 73
psychosomatic illness, 38–40
purpose. See spiritual routines
Putnam, Robert, 219

Q
Quiet: The Power of Introverts in a World
  That Can't Stop Talking (Cain), 168

R
Rawlinson, John, 214–215
reading, reflective, 182–184
reflection
 gratitude, 178–180
 integrating routines of, 190–192
 journaling, 188–190
 mindful outcomes and, 220
 prayer or meditation, 184–187
 purpose of, 177–178
 reading, 182–184
 visual focal points, 180–182
 See also spiritual routines
regret, reducing, 143
relational domain, Life GPS® and, 54
relational routines, 151–172
 building connection with, 161–172
 establishing, 112–113
 example, 195
 importance of, 151–155
 listening as, 155–160
"renouncing the fruit of your actions,"
  210–211
responsiveness, 170–172
rest and digest function, 35–36, 36,
  40–42

activating, 72
defined, 35–36, *36*
exercise for, 117–123
reversing damage with, 40–42
rewards, for routines, 111, 199–200
rhythm
    operating rhythm, 82–85
    setting boundaries, 89–92
    striving for, with routines, 107–108
Ringelmann, Danae, 75–76, 119, 197,
    216
routines, 103–114
    benefits of, 103–107
    establishing routines that last,
        109–112
    following through with, 193–203
    identifying, 72
    principles for, 107–109
    repetitive behavior for, 230
    transformation through, 47–49, 53–55
    types of, 112–113 (*See also* mental
        routines; physical routines;
        relational routines; spiritual
        routines)

S
Sarley, Dinabandhu, 72, 160
scaling back, routines and, 201–202
Seahawks (Seattle), 201
self, best version of, 51–53, *52*
self-knowledge, 61–62
self talk, 161–162, 196–197
Senior, Jennifer, 163
Servant Leadership (Greenleaf), 160
Seven Habits of Highly Effective People,
    The (Covey), 49
Shaich, Ron, 71, 173–175, 221
sleep, establishing routines for, 123–125
Slowing Down to the Speed of Life
    (Carlson, Bailey), 74, 88
Smart Brief on Leadership (January
    2012), 11
smartphones
    effect of, 8–13
    establishing routines for, 110–111

meditation timer apps for, 141
    relational routines and, 153, 163–167
"social capital," 219
Socrates, 52
Spar, Myles, 114, 120, 154, 219–220
spinal health, 127
spiritual domain, Life GPS® and, 54
spiritual routines, 173–192
    discernment and, 175–177
    establishing, 112–113
    importance of, 173–175
    reflection and, 177–192
Starner, Caroline
    on exercise, 118
    mindfulness in work of, 20, 23–24
    on peak performance, 71
    on time management techniques,
        77–79, 80, 82, 90–92, 93, 97–98
STOP technique, 134–135
story awareness, 25–27
Strategy and Business, 88
stress
    awareness of, 18
    exercise and, 118
    reaction and, 31–33 (*See also* mind-
        body operating system)
Stress Study (2013) (APA), 10–11
success, as mindful outcome, 215–218
support system
    for establishing routines, 197–198
    for exercise, 120
Swanson, Rod, 217
"sweet spot," 108
sympathetic nervous system (SNS)
    defined, 33–34
    fight or flight response and, 34, *35,*
        36, 36–38, *39*

T
tai chi, 123
Tannenbaum, Teddy, 20–21
teams
    impact of behavior on others, 96–98
    presence and, 12–13
    routines and, 110–112

telomeres, 41
Thrive (Huffington), 27
time management, 77–99
    commitment to, 79
    impact on others and, 96–98
    as intentional, 77–79
    mental routines and time frames of
        mind, 135–136, 142–146
    mindfulness about, 79–81
    necessity of tasks and, 81
    operating rhythm for, 82–85
    postponing or outsourcing for, 82
    prioritizing and, 85–87
    scheduling distractions for, 94–96
    setting boundaries and guardrails for,
        89–92
    strategic use of "yes" and "no,"
        92–94
    unconscious thought and, 88–89
    work commitment and stress, 9, *10*
transactional listening, 155–157, 158–159
transformation
    through routines, 47–49, 53–55
    transformational listening, 156–157,
        159–160
    transformational outcomes, 215–218
        (*See also* outcomes)
transient listening, 155–158
treadmill desks, 118
truth, moments of, 27–29
"tyranny of the present," 80–81
Tyson, Mike, 85

U
unconscious thought, allowing, 88–89
University of California at Irvine, 11,
    24, 94
University of California, Los Angeles, 41
University of Massachusetts Medical
    Center, 18
University of Southern California, 135
University of Wisconsin, 42
U.S. Army, 143
U.S. Coast Guard, 15–18, 21–22

V
Van Fleet, Alanson, 103–104, 141, 179,
    181–182
visual focal points, 180–182
visualization, 147
vritti, 23–24

W
Wake Forest University, 139–140
Wall Street Journal, 164
Wayt, Sian, 207–209
Wetzel, John, 59–61, 63, 216–217
Wharton School, 143. *See also* Grant,
    Adam
"what-if cycle," 232–233
Wherever You Go, There You Are
    (Kabat-Zinn), 231
Williams, Frank, 87, 118–119, 164, 169
Wingerup, Per, 83, 95, 159, 207–209
Wooden, John, 42
work arena
    Life GPS® and, 56
    mindful outcomes for, 215–218
    overworking in, 3–13
    peak performance and, 64
worry
    reflection for, 190
    uncertainty and, 223–225
    visualization for, 146–148
    "what-if cycle," 232–233

Y
"yes," strategic use of, 92–94
yoga
    benefits of, 122–123
    breathing exercises and, 41–42,
        136–137, 139–140, 143, 184–185
    Power Yoga, 19
    prana, 72–73
Young President's Organization (YPO),
    51–53

Z
"zone," being in the, 64